Social Determinants of Labour Productivity in West Africa

440 L

ACARTSOD Monograph Series - African Social Challenges

440

L **The African Social Challenges series:**

No. 1: Understanding Africa's Food Problems: Social Policy Perspectives

No. 2: The African Social Situation: Crucial Factors of Development and Transformation

No. 3: Social Development in Africa: Strategies, Policies and Programmes after the Lagos Plan

Social Determinants of Labour Productivity in West Africa

AUSTIN N. ISAMAH
Senior Research Fellow
ACARTSOD

Published for the

African Centre for Applied Research
and Training in Social Development
(ACARTSOD)

HANS ZELL PUBLISHERS
London • Melbourne • Munich • New York • 1991

Hans Zell Publishers
An imprint of Bowker-Saur Ltd, a Reed International Books Company.
Borough Green, Sevenoaks, Kent, England TN15 8PH

Published for the African Centre for Applied Research andTraining in Social Development (ACARTSOD), PO Box 80606, Tripoli, Libyan Arab Jamahiriya.

British Library Cataloguing in Publication Data

Isamah, Austin N.
Social determinants of labour productivity in West Africa. - (African social challenges, 3).
1. Personnel. Productivity
I. Title II. African Centre for Applied Research and Training in Social Development
331.118

ISBN 0-905450-48-5

Library of Congress Cataloging-in-Publication Data

Social determinants of labour productivity in West Africa / Austin N. Isamah.
189p.22cm. -- (ACARTSOD monograph series. African social challenges : no. 3)
Includes bibliographical references.
ISBN 0-905450-48-5
1. Labor productivity -- Africa, West. 2. Labor productivity -- Social aspects -- Africa, West. 3. Working class -- Africa, West. I Title. II. Series: ACARTSOD monograph series. African social challenges : 3.
HC1000. Z9L35 1990
331.11'8'0966 -- dc20 90-12851
CIP

Cover design by Robin Caira
Printed on acid-free paper.
Typeset by Kat & Mouse Typesetting, St. Clement's, Oxford
Printed in Great Britain by
Antony Rowe Ltd, Chippenham, Wiltshire

Contents

List of Figures

Foreword

Contemporary problems of underdevelopment in Africa demand that top priority be given to social development issues. There is an urgent need to identify viable options to accelerate the pace of development in this field, taking into account the specific human, cultural, and ecological conditions prevailing on the continent. The need to establish a specialised organ to deal with these and related problems was recognised by the United Nations Economic Commission for Africa (UNECA), which took the initiative of recommending the establishment of the African Centre for Applied Research and Training in Social Development (ACARTSOD).

Resolution 195(XIII) endorsing the establishment of ACARTSOD was adopted by the UNECA Conference of Ministers at its 191st meeting on 28 February 1977. This decision was endorsed in June 1977 at the 14th session of the Organisation of African Unity (OAU) Assembly of Heads of State and Government. The Centre became operational in 1980, with headquarters in Tripoli, Socialist People's Libyan Arab Jamahiriya. The Centre's main objectives include original research focusing on the identification and analysis of social development problems; the organisation of training seminars and workshops at national, sub-regional, and regional levels; the communication of the results of these activities to African governments to assist them in the formulation and implementation of social development policies and programmes; and the dissemination of research findings and publications to universities and other institutions of higher education.

In accordance with its mandate, ACARTSOD has so far produced two major categories of publications: the Research Series, which consists of studies dealing with critical social problems in Africa; and the Training Series, which comprises proceedings of seminars and other pedagogical material. The Centre has now taken another initiative by inaugurating the *African Social Challenges* Monograph Series. Publications in the series are derived from research undertaken by ACARTSOD Senior Social Development Research Fellows, commissioned research, proceedings of the annual regional workshops organised by the Centre at its headquarters, and from the best of the unsolicited manuscripts submitted to ACARTSOD by independent scholars and addressing major social development problems in Africa. Each monograph in the series is intended to have an impact on the resolution of social development problems in Africa by producing practical recommendations for action.

Africa is experiencing severe social and economic crises that threaten to rend the very fabric of society. The *African Social Challenges* Monograph Series has been established in response to these crises, and offers a contribution to the debate on how to ensure that African economies and societies are put firmly on the path to recovery and transformation. Africa must at all costs avoid a systemic breakdown by vigorously pursuing policies and programmes that will bring about transformation, increase its productive base and capacity, and promote societal cohesion and social change.

Contributing to this process is an enormous task, and ACARTSOD needs the full support of its member states, the inspiration and active participation of the intellectual community in Africa and elsewhere, and the guidance of the Governing Council and specialised bodies.

On behalf of the ACARTSOD Governing Board I would like to express my appreciation and gratitude to all ACARTSOD member states, and in particular to the People's

Libyan Arab Jamahiriya, for the financial and moral support they have committed to the Centre. Their continued support will be fundamental to the Centre's ability to sustain the *African Social Challenges* Monograph Series in the future.

Professor Adebayo Adedeji
UN Under-Secretary General
Executive Secretary, UNECA
Chairman, ACARTSOD Governing Board

1 Introduction

> The average worker, I am sorry to say, wants a job in which he does not have to put forth much physical exertion - above all he wants a job in which he does not have to think.
>
> Henry Ford

The difference that exists between potential and actual levels of worker productivity is a worldwide phenomenon. That it should exist to such a significant degree in African industry demands explanation - and this should take into account historical and socio-economic factors as well as those subjective factors that influence worker performance.

This book is the result of a recent study of low-level industrial workers in three West African urban centres - Abidjan, Accra and Lagos, and the industrial sector is taken to be the key to West African economic development. Paragraph 52 of the Lagos Plan of Action states:

> Member states accord in their development plans a major role to industrialization, in view of its impact on meeting the basic needs of the population, ensuring the integration of the economy and the modernization of society. To this end and in order for Africa to achieve a greater share of world industrial production as well as attain an adequate degree of collective self-reliance rapidly, member states proclaim the year 1980-1990 Industrial Development Decade for Africa.

During the Decade, it is doubtful whether much progress was recorded in the continent's march towards the much-desired goal of industrialization. Some of the reasons for this failure are dealt with in chapter 3.

Although the focus in this volume is West Africa, it has frequently proved difficult to restrict discussion to that region alone. West Africa comprises sixteen countries, all (except Liberia) of which were former colonies of the European powers. Most of these countries attained political independence in the 1960s. More importantly, they range in size from the giant Nigeria with an estimated population of over 100 million people, to Gambia, Guinea Bissau and Cape Verde with less than 1 million. Accurate population figures are difficult to obtain in much of West Africa, and most development planning has of necessity been based on estimates. One common feature throughout the region, however, is the predominance of the rural population. According to Onyemelukwe and Filani (1983):

> On the average about 80 per cent of each country's inhabitants are in the rural sector, the rest being urban. Settlements are urban if they have more than 20,000 inhabitants, especially if the majority are in non-agricultural occupations. There is, however, a wide variation in the population share of the urban sector among West African countries. There is a range from about 15 per cent in countries like Niger, Mali and Upper Volta [Burkina Faso] to about 25 per cent in countries like Nigeria, Ivory Coast and Senegal. With the phenomenal rate of urbanization (over 5 per cent per annum) all over Africa, not least in West Africa, the relative size of the urban population has been growing visibly, and is likely to continue with progress in processes of economic modernization.

With more people moving to the towns and cities under conditions of rapid social, economic and political change, it is increasingly urgent to understand the various aspects of the urban environment. This account of industrial workers in Côte d'Ivoire, Ghana and Nigeria is a modest contribution in this direction. The comparison of these countries is an apt one as they have much in common with a number of other West African states, sharing a similar colonial heritage with respect to the pattern of urbanization and belated industrialization; similar socio-economic problems and occupational profiles associated with a rapid rate of urban growth; and comparable levels of technological and economic development. Further, the comparison has relevance for African industrial situations throughout the continent.

2 The Problem

Work behaviour has attracted and continues to attract the attention of social scientists, philosophers, theologians, trade unionists, employers and others. It is not surprising that work behaviour has generated such a high degree of interest, as the continued existence of the human species depends on its ability to produce material goods, i.e., on its ability to work. Work is a phenomenon that is fundamental to human existence and survival, an activity that Karl Marx (1867) described as 'human action with a view to the production of use value, appropriation of natural substances to human requirements'. Throughout history, people have had to come to terms with the problem of work and all known societies have had to accord strategic importance, in one form or another, to work and to workers. The crucial importance of work in all societies was further emphasized by Marx when he argued that 'It is an everlasting nature-imposed condition of human existence and therefore independent of every social phase of that existence or rather is common to every such phase.' Thus work remains a basic reality for all societies.

Throughout history, work has assumed different meanings for different people, as the following examples will illustrate. To the ancient Greeks, whose physical labour was done by slaves, work was a curse and nothing else. Physical work of any sort was detested, and work was regarded generally as 'brutalising [to] the mind, making man unfit for thinking of truth or for practicing virtue; it was a necessary material evil which the visionary elite should avoid.' To the ancient Greeks then, no matter how abhorrent, work was a basic necessity that had to be done, albeit by slaves who were in turn granted some privileges in recognition of their usefulness to society. The Hebrews, on the other hand, saw work as a painful necessity that was the product of original sin. Thus 'To work is to atone for the sin of the ancestors and to co-operate with God in the world's salvation.' Consequently both manual and intellectual work acquired dignity and value among the Hebrews, in contrast to the Greek aversion to physical labour. More recently, the Protestant Reformation is thought to have revolutionized the meaning of work in western civilization. It has influenced the modern conception of work and has succeeded in establishing work in the modern mind as 'the base and key of life'. Thus, according to Parker (1983) 'With the idea that the best way to serve God was to do most perfectly the work of one's profession, Luther swept away the distinction between religious piety and wordly activity; profession became "calling" and work was valued as a religious path to salvation.' The nineteenth-century German thinker, Max Weber, in his highly controversial *The Protestant Ethic and the Spirit of Capitalism,* linked the rise of capitalism in the west to certain elements of the Protestant Reformation. Weber believed that 'ascetic Protestantism' promoted the accumulation of capital and hence economic growth. The absence of this value was believed to be largely responsible for the non-development of western-type capitalism in the highly developed civilizations of China, India and Islam. In traditional African societies, the norm of hard work was very much in evidence and embodied in numerous sayings, proverbs and stories. Gussman's (1953) characterization of work in the traditional African society is illuminating.

> In. . .day-to-day tribal life the African worked (and still works) extremely hard when the occasion demanded. . . .Ev-

> eryone knew the work he or she had to perform. It was learned by endless practice and the manner of doing it was sanctified by tradition. . . .Work was 'the thing to do' and group ridicule served to discourage slackers. Most forms of work, too, were buttressed by ritual. Ancestral spirits were believed to be personally interested in the successful outcome of much day-to-day activity and this supernatural sanction exerted considerable influence upon each individual's readiness to put group interests [first]. . . .While work, and extremely hard work at certain times, was generally accepted with equanimity, it was rarely, if ever, undertaken for its own sake. African proverbs stressing the importance of work for material ends are many: 'A francolin lives by scratching for itself'; and 'The bush pig that lags behind is caught by the dogs' (a man suffers if he is dilatory) are illustrations of such sayings.

It is evident that in traditional African societies work assumes a meaning that is a consequence of the co-existence of spiritual and material forces. Work is spiritual in the sense that the ancestral spirits are said to be interested in the activities of the individual, and material in the sense that it is for purely utilitarian needs. Taken together, it would appear that the meaning of work for an individual in any society is a function of what Marx called the era or social phase, the culture and status within society.

Today work remains a basic necessity in all societies irrespective of levels of technological development. Much still depends on the effort of people themselves. As Onitiri (1983) has argued:

> In spite of the great scientific advances made by man [*sic.*], the standard of living of the vast majority of the world's population still depends more on man himself than on the technological aids that are now available to him. It is his will to work, his ability to find solutions to his problems, the efficiency with which he can use technological aids, his foresight in planning for the future and the wisdom he can exercise in choosing a course of action among the various

> alternatives that are available to him, that provide the central explanation of the level of living at which he subsists.

If humanity's continued survival and well-being has depended on the ability to work, the nature of work and its mode of organization has changed with each stage of human evolution. In pre-industrial societies for instance work, though often hard, monotonous and thankless, was usually embedded in reciprocity, religious practice and community norms. As such, it was often contingent, episodic and not clearly differentiated from other activities, nor were there necessarily sharp discontinuities in space or time between work and non-work. The same cannot be said of modern industrial societies. The Industrial Revolution introduced far-reaching changes that altered not only the nature and organization of work, but also the very nature of contemporary society. Industrialization meant the transition from traditional society to modern industrial society, a movement best conveyed by Tonnie's conception of *'Gemeinschaft und Gesellschaft'* or Robert Redfield's dichotomy between 'folk and urban cultures'. With regards to work, advancements in science and technology have made the development of new skills possible, and more importantly the rationalization and fragmentation of the work process. As a consequence of industrialization, a spatial and temporal separation of work from non-work has occurred. Work now takes place in certain demarcated areas or organizations of people. People are now required to spend a certain proportion of their time in work organizations in return for a wage. Work has, therefore, acquired new meanings. Industrialization, urbanization and technological advancements have all contributed to these new meanings. Much of the existing literature indicates that work has acquired a largely negative meaning, characterized by the term 'alienation'. In certain respects, the modern worker is considered alienated from work. Green (1968) argues that it is now possible to distinguish between 'work' and 'job'. According to him, work is a calling - a life-long endeavour in which an individual seeks and expresses self-identity. On the other hand, a job is a means of making a living. In Green's view, therefore, modern industrial societies have reached the point of providing mainly jobs for people, not work.

While the repercussions of the Industrial Revolution have been felt predominantly in the now-developed countries, it is also true that newly developing countries are increasingly becoming enmeshed in the requirements of industrialization. In Africa rapid economic, social and political changes have altered the old ways of doing things. More people are increasingly being employed in formal organizations in which they work alongside similarly situated individuals. The behaviour of Africans in these work organizations and their modes of adapting to the industrial way of life have become a fertile area of interest for social scientists, both foreign and indigenous. Inevitably, studies of work behaviour in Africa have had to borrow extensively from the experiences and research findings of developed countries. In the latter there is substantial support (moral and financial) for research into work behaviour. It is not surprising that a great deal of effort has been directed towards finding ways to enhance worker productivity. This is a logical outcome of the fundamental fact that human productivity, which aside from ensuring the well-being of the population, also creates wealth. Wealthy nations in the contemporary world are those nations that, through worker productivity and innovation, have been able to accumulate a great deal of surplus product. In such societies the norm of hard work is highly valued, socially approved and usually rewarded accordingly. Comparatively these nations have achieved the highest levels of output per worker.

Today African countries have entered the age of industrialization. In each country, it is easy to identify the modern manufacturing sector utilizing technological devices to transform raw materials into finished products. Yet the full benefits of industrial production have yet to be felt by most

Africans. Without doubt, Africa is the poorest continent, in spite of being so richly endowed with natural and human resources. After several decades of struggling to overcome the problems of ignorance, disease and poverty, the evidence suggests that social and economic conditions throughout most of the continent have continued to deteriorate. According to the World Bank, even those countries with good records in the 1970s now face serious difficulties and unless present policies are altered 'The economic and social transformation of Africa, which began so eagerly and effectively in the early years of independence would be halted or even reversed.' According to Carlson (1983) the reversal has already taken place and for him 'The main issue is no longer how to accelerate the process of development but rather how to decelerate the process of underdevelopment.' Other writers foresee a very bleak future for Africa in terms of social and economic development. V. S. Naipaul stated categorically that 'Africa has no future.' Similarly, Shaw (1982) predicted that, compared with the rest of the world, the African region will be worse off at the end of this century than it was in 1960.

Is there a solution to the continent's persistent problems or should Africans be fatalistic? Of course there has been no shortage of theories, explanations and proposals for achieving a turn-around. What has been lacking has been any noticeable or significant improvement in prevailing conditions. While a few short-lived 'successes' have been recorded here and there, the situation today is one of a continent on the edge of social and economic (and in many instances, political) disaster. This implies either that the continent's problems have not been correctly diagnosed or that the wrong remedies have been recommended and applied.

Africa's problems could be traced chiefly to the fact that it is under-productive. For a variety of reasons it has proved very difficult for African countries to produce enough material goods even for domestic consumption, not to mention the surplus production critical to social and economic development. Thus the self-sufficient nations of yesterday have become virtual beggar nations today. There is unanimous agreement among economists, planners and others that a major reason for this disheartening situation is low productivity in practically all sectors of economic activity. Being endowed with abundant natural resources is meaningless if productivity remains low. As Onitiri (1983) noted, if productivity is low, these resources will be frittered away by the high costs of exploiting them. Products will be imported that, with better productivity, could have been produced at home, and a substantial proportion of foreign exchange will be spent on the services of foreign technicians whose qualifications may well be inferior to those of their domestic counterparts. Thus the path to the solution of Africa's poverty problem must begin with the search for ways to increase productivity in all sectors of the economy.

This position is beginning to attract the attention of policy-makers throughout the continent. At an August 1985 meeting in Addis Ababa, African ministers of social affairs discussed, in great detail, the problem of Africa's poverty and raised certain issues that they suggested must feature prominently in any exercise to alleviate the situation. These issues were:

1 Creating jobs for rapidly increasing populations.
2 Raising worker productivity and incomes.
3 A more just and equitable distribution of national income.

This suggests that productivity is the pivotal element on which the other two issues can be based. Economic development, as Spengler (1961) suggested, entails the diversion of a nation's scarce resources and productive powers to the augmentation of its stock of productive wealth, and to the progressive enlargement of its gross and net national product of goods and services. 'Progressive enlargement' of the national product cannot occur if productivity is generally low. Unless productivity is sufficiently high, there can be little or no surplus production for reinvestment, which in turn would create additional employment opportunities. Similarly, high productivity makes it possible to create societal wealth for eventual redistribution. Again, it must be noted that any nation that truly desires social and economic development must devise ways to achieve high worker productivity. Japan and West Germany provide classic examples of countries that rose from total defeat in 1945 to the commanding heights of economic development. It should not be surprising to learn that one of the major reasons usually advanced for these modern-day economic miracles is that both countries (through various means) were able to achieve very high levels of worker productivity.

Not only is productivity linked to the creation of jobs and the provision of surplus product for redistribution, but it is also closely related to standards of living. It is no accident that countries that enjoy high living standards are those that also have high worker productivity. Conversely, those countries that are characterized by poor standards of living are those that have very low worker productivity levels.

> To some extent low productivity is an aspect of the vicious cycle of poverty in which many developing nations are trapped. Poor standards of living - bad health, lack of education, bad housing, poor transportation to and from work, bad conditions in the workplace, etc. - reduce the worker's productivity and low productivity in turn reduces the capacity of the society to improve living standards. (Onitiri, 1983)

Determining the factors for increasing worker productivity would be a very fruitful and socially relevant area for research in contemporary Africa. Increases in productivity are possible in all sectors of national economics - in agriculture, and the tertiary sector. The present study is, however, primarily interested in productivity enhancement in industry. The reasons for this will be made clear in due course. At this juncture, we will explain what productivity connotes for this study.

Productivity has been defined in various ways, depending on the problem at hand. For the present purposes, productivity is defined as 'output per employee-hour, quality considered'. If an employee produced 20 units in one hour last month and 22 identical units in one hour today, productivity has risen by 10 per cent. If 20 units were produced last month and 20 units of higher quality are produced today, productivity has also risen although the measurement in the latter case becomes more difficult. The literature usually conveys the impression that productivity depends on the activities of labour alone. Nothing could be further from the truth. Productivity is rather the result of several related factors of production - management, land, labour, capital, technology and so on. Economic planners in Africa have tended to concentrate on certain factors of production, notably capital, technology and raw materials. Without doubt, these factors are indispensable to industrial development, but the human aspect of production surely deserves more attention than it has received. Harbison and Myers (1959) argued that 'In the march towards industrialism, capital, technology and natural resources are but passive agents. The active agents are human agents.' Arguing along the same lines, Kayode (1970) suggested that only those factors that can exercise some control over performance could be said to have productivity:

> Only labour, which has the unique attribute of being able to create a gap between actual and possible levels of performance could be truly said to have productivity. Capital has not got such an influence and therefore we cannot say that capital has productivity. The possible level of output/performance of a machine is determined by its technical capacity. The machine itself cannot influence its output. But

> labour can create a gap between the actual output and the possible levels of output of the machine. The machine cannot in this sense be said to have productivity.

Of all the factors of production, therefore, labour is the pivotal element in the productivity equation. Similarly, it is the variable that can influence, positively or negatively, productivity in industry. If labour is the central element in productivity, nowhere does it deserve more attention than in sub-Saharan Africa, where industrial expansion and development is significantly hampered by a chronic shortage of investment capital. The shortage of investment capital in turn circumscribes Africa's ability to acquire up-to-date technology to transform its industrial sector. In such a situation one remedy could be the development of human capital, a phenomenon that Harbison (1964) referred to as *human resource development*. He argued that the investment in people is equally as important as investment in material things, and that a country's rate of growth is dependent as much upon the development of human resources and the rate of human capital formation as upon the rate of physical capital formation. The establishment of schools and colleges is frequently seen as the sole answer to the problem of human resource development. This is, however, only the beginning of the process. Ways must be sought to unleash the latent creativity and innovativeness of the labour force. Societal development, the profitability and efficiency of the individual firm depend on the extent to which these powers are set free. It is in recognition of this basic fact that the industrialized countries, in spite of their technological advancement, commit a great deal of time, effort and resources to worker development. These efforts have yielded notable advances in the understanding and improvement of work behaviour in industry, especially in the United States. The *scientific management approach* and the *human relations perspective* are two important results of the drive to understand the industrial worker. Despite having basically different views of the individual as a worker, these approaches share the fundamental goal of productivity enhancement in industry, and there is evidence to suggest that they have yielded some notable successes. More recently, attention has been directed at what has become known as the *'quality of working life'* of employees. This approach places emphasis on improving the conditions under which the worker lives and labours as a prerequisite to improving performance on the job. These approaches and many others, although with different emphases, have been developed and applied to industry with the basic goal of increased productivity.

Just as productivity is a consequence of several factors, so is *labour* productivity, the two major factors in this case being technical and human. The technical factors are 'technological development (the machinery and equipment employees have to work with), the quality of raw materials, the layout of the work, and methods and techniques'. There is no doubt that improvements in technology can and do lead to significant increases in productivity. Yet the evidence indicates that 'Improvement in technology is more than offset by changes for the worse on the human side of productivity, so that productivity when expected to go up actually remains the same or increases less than predicted, or even goes down.' Even though technology is crucial in industrial production, most African nations cannot afford modern technological aids. More attention, therefore, should be given to the human factors of productivity. These are the factors that relate to the individual worker, and include:

1 worker skills - both technical and attitudinal;
2 innate ability - physical and mental energy;
3 the intensity of the application of both skill and organic ability to the production process.

These factors could be reduced to ability and motivation. Ability results from knowledge and skill. Knowledge in turn is affected by education, experience, training and interest. Skill is affected by aptitude and personality as well as by education, experience, training and interest. On the other hand, motivation is the result of the interaction of forces in the workplace, social conditions of the job and individual needs. Thus the interaction of both factors, ability and motivation, influences the performance of the worker on the job. In the words of Vroom (1964):

> The effects of ability and motivation on performance are not additive but interactive. The data presently available on the question suggest something closely resembling the multiplicative relationship depicted in the following formula:
>
> Performance = F (Ability x Motivation)
>
> It follows from the formula that, when ability has low value, increments in motivation will result in smaller increases in performance than when ability has high value. Furthermore, when motivation has low value, increments in ability will result in smaller increases in performance than when motivation has a high value.

Of these two critical factors, motivation appears to be the most problematic. This is what determines the intensity with which the worker applies skills and abilities to the task in hand. It accounts partly for the reason why some workers work harder and with a stronger sense of commitment than others. In seeking ways to increase labour productivity in African industry, those factors that influence motivation - factors that exist both on and off the job - are singled out for special treatment. This focus also raises an important question: productivity for whom? Productivity enhancement is of course the primary goal of management, but may not necessarily coincide with the goals of workers. Should increased productivity only benefit the managers and owners of industry? The answer is that in looking for factors related to the worker's motivation at work, the worker's well-being is not neglected. For instance, if it is found that more money would lead to higher productivity, the worker benefits by acquiring higher purchasing power as a result of such a recommendation. Thus, all parties in the employment relationship must be seen to benefit from any suggested plans, programmes and strategies for action. The achievement of higher worker productivity levels facilitates an expansion of the industrial organization (which means more profit for the owners), creates further employment opportunities (a societal goal) and contributes to the general prosperity of the worker in the form of higher income. Concerning potential benefits for the worker, Horton and King (1981) maintained that:

> The relative productivity of individuals within a society largely determines - for most individuals in most societies - relative incomes, notwithstanding private ownership of assets, public efforts to redistribute incomes, and the many factors that can cause a divergence between productivity and earnings.

Apart from material benefits, other non-tangible factors have also been found to be related to high productivity. The primary objective here is to identify those factors that promote individual satisfaction and productivity over the above marginal subsistence and performance. Recommendations that enhance worker productivity at the expense of individual satisfaction will, in the long term, prove inadequate and costly to industrial organization and to society at large.

The focus on industrial workers in West Africa is the result of several considerations. As N. F. Dufty suggested, the study of the sociology of blue-collar workers has many facets and is important for a number of reasons:

> To the scholar its primary importance is that it provides an avenue of research for the testing of general social theory. From the standpoint of action research, studies of blue-collar workers' alienation have a bearing on the whole system of

> stress and strains to which the industrial fabric is currently being subjected. The link between worker and political sociology has implications for democracy and for political stability. Another aspect of the subject. . .the transition from a traditional to an urban society and the discipline of industrial life, is of crucial importance in economic development.

This applies to the West African industrial situation where workers occupy a strategic position within national economies, although they are numerically small. In West Africa industrial workers account for less than 10 per cent of the total labour force, yet they occupy a position in which they could actively enhance or impede national development efforts. According to Gutkind (1968) 'Much of the future success or failure of major development projects hinges on the role these workers will play in national development.'

As most industries and their employees are concentrated in the urban centres, they can exert a definite influence on political development, either directly or indirectly. A great deal of labour and industrial unrest could be avoided if adequate strategies were adopted in the management of human resources. The emergence of appropriate strategies and approaches to industrial labour in Africa is hindered by a chronic shortage of information about workers themselves. For various reasons, including inadequate funding for research, very little systematic data exists on the performance of industrial workers. The paucity of accurate information has lead to generalizations and stereotypes about workers, many of which are grossly misleading. Two examples illustrate this problem. In the literature it is fairly common to find scholars arguing that the educational level of African workers is low and that this has negative consequences for productivity. Sellassie (1980), in a paper written for the Third Conference of African Ministers of Social Affairs, argued that 'Because of its low educational level, the information absorption capacity of the African labour force is also low, with adverse effects on labour productivity and hence on the prospects of the improvement of the living conditions of the masses.'

While there might be some truth in this assertion, it is doubtful that such statements are based on any systematic survey of the educational qualifications of the labour force. They are, however, a legacy of an earlier period in the history of wage labour in Africa when most workers were indeed illiterate. The problem in African industry today may well be one in which over-educated workers have to content themselves with low-level jobs. Another example relates to the highly controversial debate about African workers as a privileged labour aristocracy. Several scholars - Huntington (1966), Arrighi and Saul (1973) - have suggested that African workers were economically well-off compared with other segments of the lower classes. Others, like Sandbrook (1977), have argued otherwise. Mafziger (1985) suggested that 'There may have been "labour aristocrats" around, but they did not comprise the bulk of wage earners; who were unskilled or semi-skilled workers with low wages.' Accurate and up-to-date data on workers would have made such time-wasting debates unnecessary, although some useful information about workers has emerged in the process. Generally, it is remarkable that very little is known about the daily lives of workers in West Africa, especially those at the lower level.

Attention here, therefore, will focus on the attitudes and behaviour of workers in the workplace. This approach is based on the assumption that an understanding of the attitudes and feelings of workers is central to the issue of improved management of human resources in industry. Sociologists, as Cohen (1966) suggests, are never interested in attitudes as a final object of enquiry but always as part of an ultimate aim of studying the structure of social conduct. Concentration on workers' attitudes enables the researcher to explain social conduct from the perspective of the workers themselves. The underlying assumption here is that workers who have favourable attitudes towards their work organization will, all other things considered, be more productive than those with negative attitudes. 'Attitudes to work' is used here to refer to the disposition towards organizational work, feelings regarding concepts of responsibility, fairness, legitimacy concerning demands and rewards of organizational duties. Conceptualized in this manner, an attitude is a predisposition to act in a certain way in response to certain stimuli. In industry, the attitudes of workers are very important to management in the formulation and implementation of plans and policies. This becomes all the more evident once it is realized that attitudes are, in a rather complex manner, related to behaviour or 'overt action'. The link between attitude and behaviour, though not a simple one, indicates that a particular attitude of an individual provides the social scientist or manager with a useful guide to likely behaviour under certain circumstances. It is, therefore, reasonable to assume that employees who have a favourable attitude towards their work organization are likely to express this feeling in higher productivity. In the final analysis, attitudes are critical to the understanding of human behaviour, as they influence the lives of everyone and affect the ways in which individuals judge and react towards other people, objects and events. Much of everyday life is governed by the attitudes, favourable or otherwise, that are held by people. Given the importance of attitudes in industry, it is not surprising to find that attitude surveys are a standard procedure in most large industrial organizations and that managements routinely devise activities calculated to create favourable attitudes. As more people are employed by formal organizations in West Africa, it is imperative that continuous efforts should be made to understand how they perceive their jobs. An issue that is related to workers' perception of work involves the manner in which the social scientist should view the industrial worker in newly developing nations.

A number of studies of West Africa have focused on industrial workers and analysed various aspects of their working lives. These studies have, however, implicitly or explicitly, had to face the dilemma of how to view the contemporary African worker. Should the African worker be compared with the worker in the modern factories of Europe and North America, or as a unique case? Peil (1972) suggests that the factory worker in a developing country can be looked at in three ways:

> In one sense, the study can provide information on the reaction of workers whose cultural background does not include large-scale industrial organizations. Modern methodology can be used to obtain data on attitudes and reactions of workers whose situation is in many ways comparable to that of early industrial workers. Secondly, one can compare these workers with operatives in modern factories in developed countries - the automobile workers of Detroit or the affluent workers of Luton. International competition provides an impetus for modern technology wherever a factory is established. Factory workers in developing countries may seem to have a high income in comparison to other adults in their own societies even though they appear badly off when compared to 'advanced' industrial workers. The third approach is to see them as a unique case, caught between traditional habits and modern demands and responding in a way that is quite different from that of either early or modern industrial workers.

In contemporary West Africa, it would be naive to view workers in industry as a unique case different from workers in the developed world. While it might have been true in the 1950s and 1960s, rapid social, economic and political changes, together with the ease of intercontinental communication, have subsequently combined to ensure that the West African industrial worker differs only slightly from those in Europe or North America. The differential exposure to advanced technology of production introduces differences between workers in the developed countries and those in the developing countries, yet the basic human needs and aspirations in industry remain the same. A large-scale study reported by David Sirota and M. Greenwood, designed to determine the differences and similarities in work goals of thousands of industrial workers in 25 countries, found that the most important goals of these workers were all concerned with opportunity for individual achievement, and secondly that occupational and national comparisons reveal remarkable similarities in the goals of workers around the world. Sirota and Greenwood reported further that, although differences among countries are relatively small, it is possible to identify country 'clusters' within which goals are nearly identical. These clusters to some extent coincide with levels of national economic development. On the basis of that comparative study, West African workers could also be viewed as similar to the early industrial workers of the advanced countries. Much of the technology used for productive activity in West African industry can be traced to an earlier period of industrial development in the advanced countries. Similarly, workers in West Africa have yet to enjoy the many benefits that workers in the developed countries enjoy, benefits that have evolved over a long period of time. Thus in many respects the West African industrial worker is perceived as having some similarity with the industrial worker of contemporary industrialized countries, while in other respects the similarity is with the industrial worker of an earlier period in history.

The poverty of most West African nations makes industrial expansion based on the acquisition of modern, up-to-date technology an almost impossible task. It would be logical, therefore, to suggest that efforts should be concentrated on improving the performance of existing industry. According to the World Bank (1981):

> Much of African industry is plagued by low productivity, under-utilized capacity and poor management. Some of these problems stem from overall incentives, but others are specific to the sub-sector of individual firms. The problems

> are sufficiently widespread to suggest concentration on improving the performance of existing industry rather than on major programmes of industrial expansion.

Accordingly, we shall focus on one of the problems raised here, that of low productivity, in the belief that a more efficient utilization of labour would contribute immensely to the performance of West African industry.

3 Conceptual Framework

Work Behaviour

There are several approaches and theories concerning work behaviour in industry. The most notable in the sociology of industry is the *scientific management approach* closely associated with the name of Frederick Taylor and the *human relations approach* that owes much to Elton Mayo and the famous Hawthorne experiments. There are also the *motivation theories* of Maslow and Herzberg among others, that have acquired widespread utility. However, attention here is focused on scientific management and human relations. Even though they have been largely abandoned, they exert a significant influence on more contemporary explanatory models.

Briefly, scientific management or 'Taylorism' as it is sometimes called, was concerned with one pathology in industry - inefficiency - which Taylor suggested afflicted both management and workers. Taylor's primary goal was, therefore, to maximize productivity for less cost to management and at the same time bring about higher rates of pay for workers. Four principles, according to Taylor, underlay scientific management: the application of science to the work process; the scientific selection and progressive development of the worker; the bringing together of science and scientifically trained workers by management; and the bringing about of a harmonious and conflict-free relationship between management and employees. Taylor's methods consisted of selecting the best person to do the job, with instructions in the most efficient method of performing the work, and extra money as an incentive to produce at a higher rate. Evidently, Taylor placed a strong emphasis on technology as a means of rationalizing work and thereby making it more efficient, and at the same time he was convinced that the worker was an 'economic man' [*sic.*] who could be paid more to maximize production.

The human relations approach on the other hand is usually regarded as a 'radical alternative' to Taylorism, in spite of the fact that both approaches share the common goal of seeking to control the worker. However, human relations exponents go beyond the crude 'economic man' assumptions of scientific management to emphasize the crucial importance of the work group of which the worker is a member. This approach suggests that social needs are of great importance in determining workers' attitudes and behaviour in industry and highlights the significance of social relationships within the factory and the operation of group norms. In the managerial approach, which stemmed from it, the key to productivity was seen to lie in happy integrated groups. However, the human relations approach had a significant shortcoming. It neglected or dismissed socially patterned motivations that derive from workers' out-of-plant experiences. On this point, Gouldner (1959) has argued that the worker brings to the job situation a whole series of 'latent roles' - age, sex, ethnic origin, religion, class background and so on - that can be called upon to interpret that situation. Thus, he claims that an adequate consideration of the nature of worker involvement in a factory will need to venture beyond the enterprise as its unit of study. Neither the scientific management approach nor the human relations school consider extra-plant factors as of great significance in influencing worker attitudes and behaviour.

As both in-plant and extra-plant factors are closely linked, any serious analysis should consider them together.

To feature only one sphere would lead, at best, to incomplete or partial explanation. This point is particularly relevant to the situation in West Africa where the industrial way of life is yet to become all-pervasive and where the community exerts a strong influence on industry and its participants. For a comprehensive explanation of industrial behaviour in West Africa, a conceptual framework is required that takes into consideration the 'work-community nexus'. The *social action perspective* serves this purpose admirably. Action approaches attempt to explore the work-community linkage and 'to incorporate socially generated and distributed aims, attitudes and actions in the model of the worker and explanation of work behaviour'. It would be a futile exercise to seek the explanation of West African work-related behaviour solely within the work organization as some studies have attempted to do. The environment of these industrial establishments greatly influences the attitudes and actions of workers.

The social action perspective that underlies the present study derives largely, but not exclusively, from the writings of the German sociologist Max Weber (1964). According to Weber:

> In action is included all human behaviour when and insofar as the acting individual attaches a subjective meaning to it.. ..Action is social insofar as, by virtue of the subjective meaning attached to it by the acting individual...it takes account of the behaviour of others and is thereby oriented in its course.

Individuals act in accordance with their own definitions of the situation. For the sociologist interested in studying human behaviour in any setting, this demands not only that the typical social actions of typical social actors be determined, but also the *meanings* that actors typically attribute to their actions, i.e., an examination of socially distributed subjective motivations is regarded as an essential part of any analysis of patterned conduct. This does not exclude but precedes an examination of the individual psychology of the motivations of particular individuals.

Talcott Parsons (1951) further elaborated this approach to the study of human action and his argument can be summarized as follows:

1 action is goal-directed (or has an end);
2 action takes place in a situation where some elements are utilized by the actor as means to the goal;
3 action is normatively regulated with respect to the choice of ends and means.

For the individual, action has an end or a goal, and is rational, though from the perspective of an observer, such action might seem irrational. This implies that the observer or social scientist involved in a different social situation from his or her own must try to understand the actions of those people being observed or studied from *their* perspectives, from their subjective interpretations of the situation. A classic example of the failure of scholars to follow this basic rule is the fact that in the majority of earlier writings about labour in Africa, the reluctance of Africans to come out of their villages to embrace wage employment was interpreted by European and American scholars as irrational. Yet, as is now evident, the actions of those Africans were based on a purely rational calculation of the costs and benefits of wage employment and the conclusion that (at least in the early days of wage employment on the continent) the costs far outweighed the potential benefits. Action, as already pointed out, takes place in a situation that Parsons divided into two: those situations over which the actor has no control, cannot alter or prevent from being altered to fall in line with the sought end; and those situations over which the actor has such controls. Those conditions that could not be controlled were termed the 'conditions' of action and those that could be controlled, the 'means'. The existence of a choice of alternative means to an end creates room for normative orientation of action. Thus, the means that the actor chooses (within the area of control) is not chosen at random nor is it dependent exclusively on the conditions of action. Rather, this choice is a function of an independent, determinate selective factor. The actor has been influenced by this factor in making a choice. What the social action perspective suggests is that any instance of action (a unit act) stems from the ends that the actor is concerned to attain, the definition of the situation. This includes the range of alternative actions that are perceived to be available and the choice of means that are likely to be effective, bearing in mind the likely reactions of others. The meaning on which the actor grounds the interpretation and definition of the situation derives from experience in the community. These meanings derive generally from what Durkheim (1895) called 'social facts'. According to Durkheim social facts refer to:

> every way of acting, fixed or not, capable of exercising on the individual an influence, or an external constraint, or again, every way of acting which is general throughout a given society, while at the same time existing in its own right independent of its individual manifestations.

In any society, the typical social facts are laws and customs, the content of education and currents of opinion. All these constitute the culture of a particular people and account for the fact that, while each individual behaves in a unique manner, some form of uniformity of behaviour is discernible for groups or an entire society. The social action perspective is suitable here, as it takes consideration of external factors in addition to internal factors in explaining workers' behaviour at work. Mannel's (1974) summary of the theory of action is very much in order here.

> Firstly, people's actions are directed towards the achievement of ends, goals, objectives. Secondly, people select appropriate means and procedures from those available to

> attain their ends. Thirdly, courses of action are constrained by the conditions of the physical and social environment. Fourthly, individuals have emotions and make moral judgements which influence the selection of ends and means as well as their order of priority. Finally, actions are to be explained by the subjectively intended meaning given to them by the actor or roughly by [the actor's] perception and definition of the ends, means and conditions of [the] situation.

The action approach has been fruitfully applied to the study of work behaviour from the late 1960s by British and French researchers, though several writers have noted that it had 'existed in industrial sociology long before it was systematically propounded and consciously advocated'. It was J. H. Goldthorpe and his associates in their 'Affluent Workers' studies who brought the approach firmly into mainstream industrial studies. They advocated the use of a

> frame of reference within which the actors' own definitions of the situation in which they are engaged are taken as an initial basis for the explanation of their social behaviour and relationships...(which) would direct attention systematically to the variety of meanings which work may come to have for industrial employees.

The argument is that the starting-point for analysis should be 'with the ordering of wants and expectations relative to work, and with the meaning thus given to work' and that a 'key explanatory notion' was 'the definition of work and of the work situation' of the workers studied. The workers' orientation to work and employment was to be regarded as 'a crucial independent variable relative to what occurs in the work situation' so as to account for its involvement in investigating non-work aspects of the social lives of the workers concerned.

Thus the lasting contribution of Goldthorpe and his associates to the study of workplace behaviour is their emphasis on an understanding of the employee's orientation to work as a prior step to understanding subsequent behaviour in the workplace. Not surprisingly, the concept of 'orientation to work' has featured prominently in subsequent studies, and has been defined in various ways. However, for our purposes we agree with Benett (1974) that the concept should mean some reflection of representation of the total motivational state of an individual at a point in time, thus portraying the effects of needs, values, attitudes, abilities and other behavioural aspects. Defined operationally, it is 'an expression of how an individual views [a] situation in terms of what [one] desires from it and the extent [to] which [one] expects these desires to be achieved or not'.

Several types of 'orientation to work' have been identified. Goldthorpe *et al.* (1968) distinguished three types - instrumental, solidaristic and bureaucratic. Workers with an instrumental orientation see work almost exclusively as a means of acquiring an income necessary to support a valued way of life. They have a calculated relationship to the employing organization, are not involved in their jobs and usually make a sharp distinction between work and non-work. A bureaucratic orientation involves service to an organization in return for a career, positive involvement in work and the organization, and no sharp distinction between work and non-work. Workers with solidaristic orientation are seen as experiencing work as a group activity that may lead either to identification with the firm, or with the work group as a source of power against the employer. Social relationships and shared activities at work are found rewarding and work relationships in some cases form the basis of occupational communities outside work. Largely based upon the typology developed by Goldthorpe and associates, other types of orientation to work have been identified and include those of Benett (1978), Ingham (1967, 1970) and Silverman (1970).

From the discussion so far, it is possible to identify a social action model of explanation as an analytical framework. As figure 3.1 indicates, personal background factors and current situational factors (including the local culture, educational experiences, etc.) determine what type of orientation the individual has towards the job. This orientation is, however, mediated by specific organizational and job factors that either cause high motivation leading to job efficiency or low motivation leading to slacking.

Thus the conceptual framework adopted here takes cognizance of the social background and experiences of the worker, in addition to the influence of specific job factors and role in the organization. The interaction of both sets of factors determine the individual's satisfaction or dissatisfaction with the job. If aspirations, wants and expectations are realized by membership in the organization, it is reasonable to expect that there will be job satisfaction and a favourable view of management's goal of high productivity. If aspirations and expectations cannot be fulfilled by the job, motivation will be minimal and manifested by lacklustre performance.

Statement of Hypotheses

Given the direction of the discussion so far, we would adopt the general hypothesis that in the particular social context of West African industry, a worker's performance will depend on the degree of satisfaction derived from the job, and that a direct and positive relationship exists between job satisfaction and performance. Accordingly, it would be expected that the stronger the feeling of satisfaction, the greater acceptance of management's goal of higher productivity and profitability. Conversely, the dissatisfied worker will manifest hostility in numerous subtle ways, and exhortations from management and other interested parties for higher productivity in the interests of the company and nation will have little or no effect.

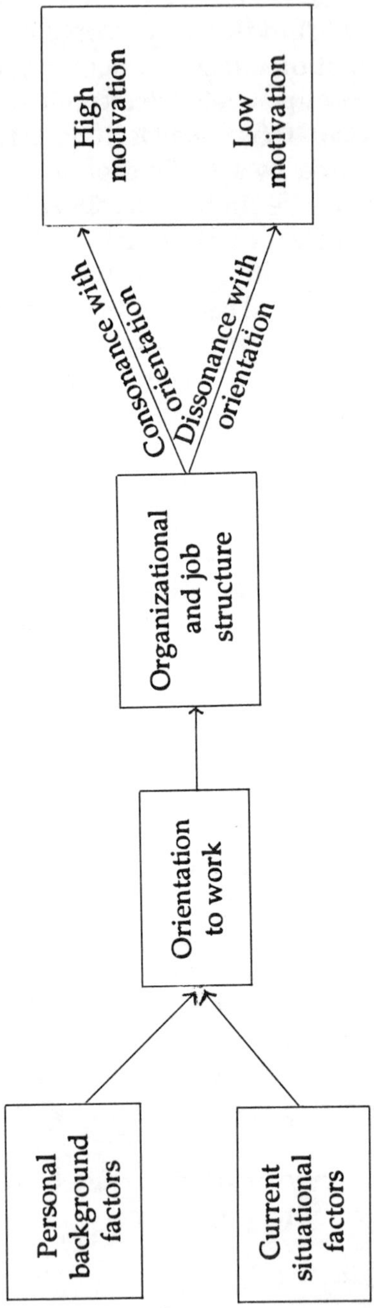

Figure 3.1 A social action model

Workers' performance was found to be affected by other factors as well. For our purposes, we identify two - autonomy and control of the work process. Workers who have some freedom to decide the way they do their jobs are said to perform better than those who do not. Similarly, close supervision and lack of participation was found to lead to poor performance. Workers who have some measure of control over the work process will tend to perform better than those whose work process has been so rationalized as to require no input from them except to operate the machines. Thus, the more worker control, the higher the performance. Similarly, performance will be higher where employees have some power to influence decisions that affect their immediate job environment. Job performance will be higher in firms where some authority to influence decisions is delegated to employees than in firms where authority is concentrated in management hands.

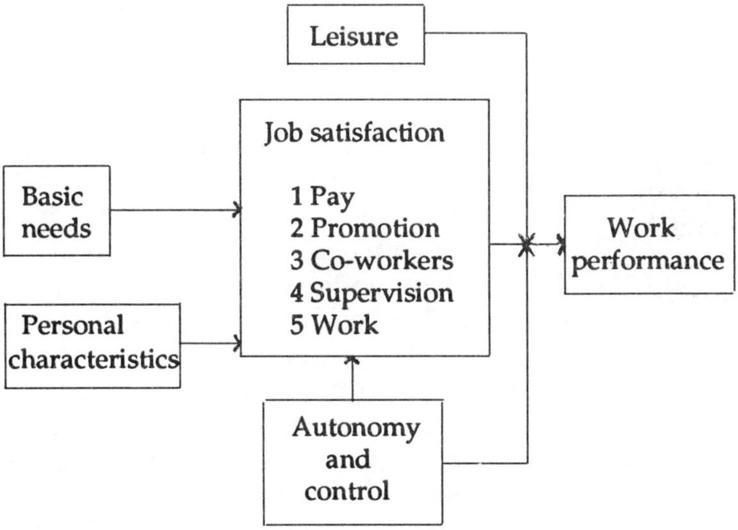

Figure 3.2 Factors affecting work performance

Job satisfaction and work performance are also affected by extra-plant factors. Job satisfaction is enhanced or mitigated by the worker's personal characteristics such as age, sex, educational background and place of birth. From this we derive several specific hypotheses: the older the worker, the more job satisfaction; educated workers performing semi-skilled jobs will be less satisfied than uneducated workers performing the same tasks; workers from rural areas will tend to be more satisfied with a factory job than urban-socialized workers; Finally, workers whose jobs fulfill their basic needs will report higher job satisfaction.

Performance has also been found to vary with the amount and type of leisure that the employee enjoys. Thus we want to hypothesize that the more leisure activities the employee enjoys, the higher the performance, as illustrated in figure 3.2.

Several concepts that recur frequently in this study require explanation and it is to this that we turn next.

Work Performance

The concept of performance is used here interchangeably with productivity. Both refer to how efficiently and effectively a worker carries out a task when judged against an existing standard in the organization. Thus a worker who produces 70 units in one hour is said to demonstrate a higher level of performance than another worker who produces 60 units in the same time. The basic assumption is that there is usually a discrepancy between potential output and actual output in industry and with the right diagnosis and prescription this gap could be bridged. Thus work performance refers not only to how hard an individual works but also how total responsibilities are discharged on the job. Measurement of work performance is obtained by means of an eight-item performance evaluation format derived from company employee appraisal exercises. Each item is graded from 'outstanding' through 'average' to 'below average'. The maximum score for each employee is 32 while the minimum is 8.

Job Satisfaction

This is a fairly common concept in sociological and psychological studies of work behaviour and reflects the general attitude of an employee to the job. Here it is regarded as indicating the degree to which the employee feels rewarded and fairly treated in the job. As noted earlier, it is strongly mediated by external factors that include the employee's personal background. In the contemporary literature, especially that concerning employees in the industrial societies, the relationship between job satisfaction and productivity is regarded as tenuous at best. However, for the comparatively uncomplicated situation in Africa, we maintain that the relationship is positive and significant. Brayfield and Crochett (1955) were correct when they suggested that

> [the] hypothesis that production should increase monotonically with increases in satisfaction apparently rests on the assumption that the worker will demonstrate. . .gratitude by increasing output, or that increased satisfaction frees certain creative energies in the worker, or that the satisfied employee accepts management's goals which include high production.

They conclude that, in any event, it is commonly hypothesized that whatever the cause, increased satisfaction makes workers more motivated to produce.

Job satisfaction is measured by a modified form of the Job Descriptive Index (JDI). The index comprises a series of items broadly divided into the following dimensions:

1 satisfaction with pay;
2 satisfaction with work;
3 satisfaction with opportunities for promotion;

4 satisfaction with supervision;
5 satisfaction with co-workers.

The maximum score for a very satisfied employee is 195 while the minimum is 0 for a very dissatisfied employee.

Alienation

Alienation has become a recurrent concept in the literature as industrialization becomes the dominant way of life. It is a concept that derives largely from the writings of Karl Marx. Marx believed that 'Work provided the most important and vital means for man to fulfil. . .basic needs. . .individuality and. . .humanity. By expressing. . .personality in the creation of a product, the worker can express a deep satisfaction.' Modern work organization under capitalism, however, makes the achievement of this satisfaction increasingly difficult, hence the worker is said to be alienated. Alienation is thus defined as 'disconnection, separation - the process by which human beings are cut adrift from their natural moorings in the world as the result of unnatural, alien work arrangements'. The increasing rationalization of work and the decreasing control of the worker over the work situation are the two major sources of alienation in industry. They function to render the worker powerless and hence dissatisfied with work. It is important to note that alienation in the form of powerlessness is not limited to the workplace but can be found in all aspects of capitalist society. Thus it is possible that the worker, in addition to being alienated on the job, is also alienated from the political sphere of the community.

Leisure

Increasing industrialization has made a sharp dichotomy between work and non-work possible. During non-work time the worker is free to pursue certain activities, some of which can be regarded as leisure. Leisure refers to a freely chosen, uncommitted occupation of the individual's time on activities that s/he finds rewarding and fulfilling. Thus 'True leisure activity is. . .freely chosen and pursued at the moment and in the way desired by the individual concerned, who expects from it satisfaction and even a certain inner growth.' Clearly then, leisure activities constitute only one aspect of the range of activities that the worker pursues after work.

Leisure has become increasingly important to the modern worker as more rationalization of work takes place and as less satisfaction is derived from the job. Leisure could function as a compensatory factor providing 'relaxation from tension' or 'recuperation from the strains' inherent in modern work organization. In the words of Georges Friedman (1961) 'The worker seeks to regain in. . .leisure hours the initiatives, responsibility and sense of achievement denied [in work].' The argument here is that the worker would perform 'reasonably well' at a dull and monotonous job if after-work activities were more interesting and satisfying.

Basic Needs

All human beings have certain fundamental needs that must be met for continued survival. As the motivation theory of Abraham Maslow suggests, when these primary needs are met, other needs develop and these are what motivate individuals to act. The theory suggests that the needs of individuals could be arranged in a hierarchy from the lowest to the highest. Sutermeister (1976) divides the needs of the worker into three broad groups - physiological needs (for food, clothing, shelter, etc.), social needs (for friendship, love, etc.) and egoistic needs (for achievement, fulfilment, and so on). The worker will tend to express satisfaction if very important needs are satisfied by the job and be dissatisfied if only part of these important needs are satisfied. Evidence in West Africa points to the fact that workers are still very much concerned with basic physiological needs, and it makes no sense to divert attention to the higher needs when the more fundamental ones are yet to be fulfilled.

Method

Data for this study was obtained through two major sources: first, through a questionnaire survey of a selected sample of factory operatives in three West African capital cities - Accra, Abidjan and Lagos.[1] The objective of the survey was to compare the responses of these three groups of employees so that, in the final analysis, acceptable generalizations could be made about industrial workers in West Africa. The questionnaire schedule was specifically designed for low-level factory workers directly involved in production, and measures their attitudes to work and to life in general. This category of employees is of particular interest since their level of performance is of primary importance to most managers. Secondly, another set of data was collected from key management personnel through the use of a structured interview schedule. As with the questionnaire schedule, the interview schedule was standardized for the three cities. This was designed primarily to obtain information on different aspects of workplace organization such as hierarchy of authority, type of technology used, size of workforce and so on. The performance evaluation format, which recorded aspects of each employee's performance on the job, was compiled from company records. Finally, wherever possible, informal interviewing and observation of the employees, both on and off the job, were undertaken in order to supplement, as far as was possible, the data obtained from the questionnaire schedule. This proved very successful, as many workers were very communicative about their experiences and feelings, both about their jobs and about life in general.

There is no doubt that increasing numbers of West Africans are becoming involved in wage employment.

Although the proportion of wage-earners in the region's workforce is still small, there is every indication that it will continue to increase steadily, as it has between 1960 and 1979. In Ghana, Côte d'Ivoire and Nigeria the industrial workforce was comparatively small in 1979 (20 per cent, 4 per cent and 18 per cent of the total workforce, respectively) yet in the major cities of West Africa industrial labour constitutes an important social category.

In each of the cities visited, a list of manufacturing establishments employing more than 100 employees was compiled. Using predetermined criteria, one establishment was selected in each city. The three firms chosen share several common features: they produce similar products, are import-substituting concerns and they use similar technology, mainly of an assembly-line type.

The Sample

The sample in each of the three organizations was selected from a sampling frame of all production employees that was supplied by the personnel department in each case. All employees who were not directly involved in production were eliminated from this sample frame, and self-administered questionnaires were distributed (250 in Accra, 250 in Abidjan, and 400 in Lagos) on a simple random basis, to the remaining operatives. The percentage of returned questionnaires (73.6 per cent in Accra, 69.2 per cent in Abidjan) was quite adequate, though it was comparatively low in Lagos (54 per cent). This fact is of interest in itself as it could indicate higher labour turnover or lower worker involvement in Lagos.

The analysis of collected data used primarily uncomplicated statistical techniques, as the study was largely an exploratory one. However, in the course of discussion, tests of association were employed in addition to basic frequency distributions, at appropriate points.

The Factories

In each of the cities visited the objective was to select a typical industrial establishment from which a sample of industrial employees could be drawn. Given the prevalence of West African import-substitution industrial firms engaged in the manufacture of consumer items, it was only logical that the 'typical' factory be chosen from this category of concerns. The three factories eventually selected in Lagos, Accra and Abidjan were of medium size and engaged in the production of similar consumer items, using assembly-line technology. Technology is a very crucial element of modern industrial activity, and a number of social scientists believe it to be the most important single factor that gives an industry a distinctive character. Technology, according to Blauner (1964), refers to the complex of physical objects and technical operations (both manual and machine) regularly employed in producing the goods and services of an industry. Technology signifies the machine system, the level and type of mechanization as well as the technical 'know-how' and mechanical skills involved in production. The technology of modern industry is the most important single determinant of who does what kind of work, when and in what manner. Thus any significant analysis of modern work must recognize the pervasive influence that technology has on all its aspects. Assembly-line technology represents one of the most significant advancements in the field of technological development. Woodward (1958) identified three main types of technology in modern industry:

1 small batch and unit production;
2 large batch and mass production;
3 process production.

> It will be seen that the systems of production given (above) form a scale; they are listed in order of chronological development and technical complexity; the production of unit

> articles to customers' individual requirements being the oldest and simplest form of manufacture, and continuous flow production of dimensional products, the most advanced and most complicated. (Woodward, 1958)

The large batch and mass production system is the most common in developing areas such as West Africa. In these types of factories, large quantities of commodities are produced with the aid of 'conveyor-belt assembly-line' technology. Although this is a highly rationalized and fragmented system of production, it does make the efficient production of large quantities of goods possible. Perhaps the most common epitome of this system of production is automobile assembly. The same process has been applied to the production of basic consumer commodities. Essentially, the assembly-line system of production involves 'an uninterrupted series of elementary tasks, each having a limited duration and accompanied by a progression of the object in the course of its fabrication. Henry Ford, the first man to apply the assembly-line technique to automobile manufacture, described some of the features of the assembly line thus:

> Every piece of work in the shop moves; it may move on hooks, on overhead chains going to assembly in the exact order in which the parts are required; it may travel on a moving platform or it may go by gravity, but the point is that there is no lifting or trucking of anything other than materials.

This is an apt characterization of the assembly line. In the factories visited, workers involved in direct production are strung out along the platform line performing some task or another while the belt moves on. However, one factor must be mentioned. The speed of the belt varied in the three factories. In the Lagos factory, the speed was much faster than in the other two factories. The speed of the belt is dependent on several factors: the availability of raw materials, the market for the finished product and the goals of management. The Lagos factory had a greater demand for its products than either of the other two, so the management insisted on a higher speed for the conveyor-belt. The assembly line can be linked to that identified by Georges Friedman, which he called *'chaînes tendues'*, where work is fast, tense, strained and nervous. The situation in the other two factories, especially in Accra, approximated the *'chaînes sociales'* where the pace is more relaxed.

However, the subdivision of work into small parts, as observed in these factories, has one major advantage. It leads to specialization on the part of the operative. By doing the same thing every day one becomes a specialist in that task. Each person must fulfill responsibilities if the overall job is to be done, creating a high level of interdependency. Charles Babbage noted some of the advantages of worker specialization as far back as 1832. These are: ease of training - a worker can be trained to carry out one or two specific operations faster than an apprentice can be trained in all the operations required to manufacture a product; less loss of time - by reducing movement from one operation to another and from one tool to another; greater skill - by carrying out a specific operation repeatedly, workers develop greater dexterity and speed of movement; improvement in methods - by devoting their entire effort to one operation, engineers are able to simplify and improve production methods; and finally, selection of labour - workers can be selected for the operations for which they are best suited.

Even though the specialization involved in the assembly-line production system has important advantages, several disadvantages have also been identified. The most important is alienation of the worker. Drucker (1950) suggests that overspecialization is not an inevitable consequence of mass production and that 'The traditional assembly line is simply a piece of poor engineering judged by standards of human relations as well as those of production efficiency and output.' He argued further that there is evidence that the use of the worker as a single-purpose tool is a wasteful use of an individual in the production process. 'It is poor engineering that leads to tension, frustration and dissatisfaction.' These are the features of assembly-line technology that concern us here, as they are directly or indirectly linked to worker productivity. For now, however, the major point is that the conveyor-belt assembly-line system of production characterizes the three factories from which the sample of workers was chosen.

Recent research has found that technology strongly influences the shape of the organizational structure. According to Woodward (1962) 'Research revealed that firms using similar technical methods had similar organizational structure. It appeared that different technologies imposed different kinds of demands on individuals and organizations and that these demands had to be met through appropriate forms of organization.' This was found to be correct, with minor variations, for all three factories. The dominant form of organizational structure was the hierarchical arrangement of clearly defined positions from the Board of Directors to the manual (casual) labourers. In these factories there are specialized divisions involved in different aspects of the task. There are administrative divisions, production divisions, finance divisions and sales or marketing divisions, all headed by their respective middle managers who report to the top managers. Similarly, at the lower levels, positions are graded from unskilled to supervisory levels. However, in the three factories, semi-skilled operatives form the largest single categories.

Ownership is another important feature of these factories. The Lagos factory is part of a large, privately owned conglomerate involved in many areas of consumer item production. The Lagos factory is one of four similar factories making the same product, although the other three factories are spread out throughout the country. In conformity with the stipulations of the Nigerian Indigenization Decree of 1974, 40 per cent of the company's shares are held by foreign interests, with the remaining 60 per cent held by Nigerian shareholders. The factory is located on an industrial estate, which is now to be found within the city proper as a result of the city's tremendous rate of expansion. In terms of management, there are two divisions: first, the central management group that co-ordinates the activities of the three factories. This group is different from the factory management itself. Here there is a factory manager, to whom all other specialist managers are responsible. The expatriate presence is limited to the production section while all other employees are indigenous personnel. Industrial unrest has been a fairly common occurrence in the past. More recently, however, it has been minimal, as the scarcity of alternative employment has increased the fear of job loss as a consequence of industrial conflict. This is not limited to the Lagos factory alone. Statistics from the Federal Ministry of Labour and Productivity indicate a significant drop in worker hours lost through industrial unrest in the past few years.

The Accra factory, the oldest of the three, was established in the late 1950s and originally owned privately by a business man in conjunction with some foreign partners, who were the owners of the brand name. The factory has since been taken over by the state, although it is still being run along private-sector lines. It is located on the outskirts of Accra and the Managing Director is the only expatriate among the personnel. This factory has encountered serious difficulties in obtaining raw materials and spare parts for machines. Although the situation had improved somewhat at the time of the study, a cursory observation shows that the difficulties are far from over. On the other hand, such difficulties are minimal in the Abidjan factory. This is the factory with the most substantial foreign participation. Like the Lagos factory, the Abidjan factory is part of a multinational corporation that is involved in making the same product in other French-speaking countries - Cameroon, Senegal, Mali and Togo. It is located in the industrial zone of Abidjan and is the newest of the three factories under comparison. The factor that differentiates it from the other two is the predominance of expatriates at management level: expatriates form 60 per cent of all managers, although the Chairman of the Board is Ivorian. Partly as a consequence of this expatriate predominance, the hierarchy of authority is steeper than that found in the Lagos or Accra factories, and similarly income differentials are wider here too. Taking all these factors into account, it is evident that the three factories selected in Lagos, Abidjan and Accra are similar in many respects, notably in terms of the product manufactured and the technology used. As noted earlier, the assembly-line production system largely determines the organizational structure, which is hierarchical with very clearly defined positions. These factors are very important in the determination of employee performance, especially when linked with the orientations that the employees bring to the work situation.

Notes

[1] Four cities - Accra, Abidjan, Dakar and Lagos - were visited and questionnaires given to selected workers, but it proved impossible to recover the questionnaires from the Dakar sample, despite concerted efforts to do so. The reasons for failure were not clear, but may have involved bureaucratic as well as other factors.

4 Industrialization in West Africa

The industrialization process represents one of the most significant advances in the history of humankind. Centuries of innovation and creativity culminated in what is now known as the Industrial Revolution, which originated in Great Britain and spread around the world. Its significance is so great that it has come to be regarded as an indispensable variable in any nation's attempt to develop and modernize. Essentially, the concept refers to the replacement of animate sources of power, used in productive activity, with machine power. However, industrialization has come to connote much more. The United Nations Committee on Industrial Development in 1963 defined it as:

> a process of economic development in which a growing part of the natural resources is mobilised to develop a technically up to date, diversified economic structure characterised by a dynamic manufacturing sector having and producing means of production and consumer goods and capable of assuring a high rate of growth for the economy and of achieving economic and social progress.

This definition implies a great deal of social change for the industrializing society. Indeed it implies the transition from a traditional society to an industrial one with concomitant changes in social values and institutions. As Miller and Form (1964) stated:

> It is often overlooked that the revolution in manufacturing which gained impetus in eighteenth century Western Europe was preceded by changes in the values of the societies that composed it. While many different values became modified, the underlying change was the innovation of rational thought into many areas previously considered sacred. The area which felt the greatest application of rational systems of thought was economics, particularly in manufacturing. In an interdependent society all other social institutions had to make corresponding adjustments. In this particular sense, we can think of the industrial revolution as creating an industrial society.

The changes engendered by the Industrial Revolution have been fully realized in the advanced industrial societies, which today are regarded as the developed societies of the world. Smelser (1966) isolated several interrelated technical, economic and ecological processes that frequently accompany development:

1 in the realm of technology, the change from simple and traditional techniques towards the application of scientific knowledge;
2 in agriculture, the evolution from subsistence farming towards commercial production of agricultural goods - this means specialization in cash crops, purchase of non-agricultural products in the market, and often agricultural wage labour;
3 in industry, the transition from the use of human and animal power towards industrialization proper, or 'men aggregated at power-driven machines, working for monetary return with the products of the manufacturing process entering into a market based on a network of exchange relations';
4 in ecological arrangements, the movement from the farm and village towards urban centres. While these changes have largely been realized in the developed societies, they

are still underway in Africa as in other parts of the developing world.

The concern here is specifically with industry and the industrialization process, although it is difficult to overlook the accompanying changes. Industrialization is held to refer to manufacturing, the mechanical or chemical transformation of organic or inorganic materials into new products, which is carried out in factories. For developing countries the transformation of economic activities entailed by industrialization is an ultimate objective towards which much energy and resources have been directed. The advantages of a successful industrialization drive for these newly modernizing nations include the expansion of employment opportunities, self-reliance in domestic production, and a significant boost in foreign exchange earnings. Translated into social terms, this means higher living standards, but a more fundamental logic underlies the pursuit of industrialization by developing nations. The evidence available seems to indicate that industrialization has become a prerequisite for development in the contemporary world. Thus Bhagavan (1979) argued that:

1 countries cannot achieve high per caput incomes and living standards without industrialization;
2 rising incomes in turn lead to increasing demand (income elasticity of demand) for industrial goods that soon outstrips those for non-industrial goods;
3 countries cannot become wealthy and independent even in the long term without first becoming substantially industrialized.

The point here is not to underplay or underemphasize the role of agricultural production in national development, especially among developing countries in Africa. However, the development process cannot begin in these countries if efforts are concentrated solely on rural and agricultural development - the implication is that any gains in rural production can only be sustained by simultaneous progress in industrial activities. Both sectors should supplement and complement each other. Thus industry can assist agricultural productivity in the following ways:

1 by manufacturing fertilizers and pesticides, as well as farm tools, equipment and machinery at appropriate levels of technology;
2 by processing agricultural raw materials; preserving foodstuffs and transforming fibres into clothes and other manufactures to increase domestic consumption and to augment their export value;
3 by increasing the availability of low-priced consumer necessities, thereby providing incentives for peasants to increase their output;
4 by creating jobs for labourers released from agriculture as productivity rises.

On the other hand, increased agricultural productivity should assist industrial growth by:

1 providing raw materials for domestic industries;
2 producing foodstuffs for industrial workers;
3 expanding exports to earn foreign exchange to buy machinery and equipment;
4 releasing additional labour for the expanding industrial sector.

The close relationship between agriculture and industry notwithstanding, the evidence seems to suggest that the preeminent position be assigned to industrial production if real social and economic development is to take place. It is not surprising that at independence most African countries assigned priority in terms of effort and resources to the goal of industrialization, and some impressive gains were recorded in the early years of political independence in much of the continent. Between 1960 and 1965, the industrial productivity growth rate for the whole continent averaged over 10 per cent. Unfortunately, this could not be sustained and consolidated, and from 1965 to 1975 the growth rate averaged less than 5 per cent. The situation has deteriorated further since 1975 and much of the earlier optimism about industrializing the continent has all but evaporated - indeed, in most government circles there is a palpable disenchantment with the industrial sector. However, Streeten (1984) has argued that this disenchantment 'with industrialization in recent writings and speeches has been based on confusion; it is disenchantment with the form that economic growth has taken in some developing countries and with the distribution of its benefits'. There is nothing wrong with industrialization *per se*, but with the *type and nature* of the industrialization strategy that has emerged in parts of the developing world. The World Bank (1981) pinpointed some of the specific shortcomings of the emergent pattern of industrialization in Africa. These include: the fact that industry has tended to be a burden on agriculture rather than being supportive; has made excessive claims on scarce foreign exchange; has not generated domestic savings and government revenue as anticipated; and has not provided a sound industrial base for future growth of the sector (this would have been desirable given the high costs of stagnant productivity). What type of industrialization strategy evinces so many shortcomings?

In West Africa the emerging pattern of industrialization took the form of import substitution. A proper historical perspective is essential to an understanding of this strategy, and a brief account of the history of industrial activities in West Africa would be helpful at this point. Manufacturing in the contemporary sense is a relatively recent phenomenon in West Africa, as very little modern manufacturing existed in the region prior to the present century - the foundation of modern industrial production was laid during the colonial era. The emphasis here on *modern* manufacturing is important because colonial capitalism did not encounter a vacuum in these colonies, but rather a number of fairly vigorous local systems of hand manufacture of consumer goods and work implements, which had developed over the centuries. The basic components of these goods were different kinds of metals, woods, textiles, stones, clays and leather that were worked by professional artisans and/or artisans-cum-peasants who owned their own tools. In order for colonial capitalist activities to take root, survive and progress, many of the competing indigenous economic activities had to be undermined. We should bear in mind the fact that the whole purpose of the colonization enterprise was to secure exclusive sources of raw materials for emerging industrial establishments in the metropolitan country, create markets for cheap manufactured goods and find profitable new areas in which to invest surplus capital. Thus the economic preoccupation for much of the early colonial period was the production of agricultural and mineral commodities for export as industrial raw materials. This situation prevailed until World War II, when maritime difficulties made the importation of essential consumer items into the West African colonies a very problematic endeavour. This forced a reassessment among colonial administrators and entrepreneurs of the need to manufacture some of these imported items locally. However, events after the war produced some fairly remarkable economic activities. Post-war reconstruction and rehabilitation created a boom in demand for West African raw materials:

> The resulting global surge in effective demand for West African products gave rise to rising world prices for the region's raw materials. This meant an economic boost to West African trade with Europe and North America in particular....One important foreign exchange implication of this state of affairs was that many West African exporters suddenly found themselves financially able to invest surplus capital in new avenues which had previously remained

> inaccessible due to the absence of the right size of capital. Manufacturing on a large scale was not only seen as one such avenue, but also as the key to sustained economic transformation in each West African country. Furthermore, it was a means of maximizing the economic advantages of the post-war boom involving trade in tropical products through some form of commodity valorization. This involved first-stage processing of agricultural commodities and beneficiation of minerals in order to increase the values of those products and make them more capable of absorbing costs of long-distance transportation. (Onyemelukwe and Filani, 1983)

The first step in the industrialization of West Africa involved the establishment of processing facilities to handle raw materials that were billed for export. Simultaneously, a few manufacturing plants were established to produce goods that formerly had been imported from the metropolis. The idea was to import and use capital goods for the production of consumer goods that would otherwise have to be imported. This strategy came to be called import substitution industrialization, since it involved simply the substitution of imported finished goods with the local manufacture or assembly of the same. The underlying rationale was that by starting with 'final touch' industries a country could be led systematically by backward linkage to developing domestic production of intermediate, and then basic industrial materials. The strategy has several advantages; 'as a means of minimizing foreign exchange drainage as imports are restricted to items that cannot be made with locally available [labour] and technology', and secondly, as 'a simple approach to economic self-reliance, enabling a country to produce most consumer goods as well as some of the simpler capital goods (such as nails, paints, simple plastic materials) that otherwise have to be imported'.

The pace of this type of industrialization quickened when the majority of West African countries attained independence in the late 1950s to early 1960s, and facilitated the establishment of numerous industrial concerns throughout the region. Each country is dotted with industrial establishments producing a range of materials, mostly for internal consumption and occasionally for export. It must be emphasized, however, that the pattern of industrialization that has emerged favours the prevalence of light industry, i.e., the production of consumer items. Conversely, there is very little intermediate or heavy industrial activity in the region.[1]

In spite of the establishment of these industrial concerns, it must also be noted that the adoption of import substitution as the cornerstone of West African policy objectives has met with limited success. With the possible exception of Nigeria and perhaps Côte d'Ivoire, none of the countries in the region has progressed beyond the 'final touch' industries stage and all remain as dependent as ever on the developed countries for the importation of vital goods. This raises fundamental questions about the suitability of import substitution as an industrial development strategy for developing nations. Frank (1967) pointed out that:

> The import substitution process, instead of reducing import requirements, thus increases them. Moreover, it tends to raise the cost of imports as it becomes necessary to import ever more technically complicated, advanced, monopolised, and thus costly equipment from the metropolis. Yet this import substitution cannot reach the point at which the satellite ceases to be dependent on the metropolis for equipment, technology and critical raw materials, since this industrial blind alley leads the satellite country away from rather than toward the production of these necessities.

This inappropriate industrial strategy has had two major consequences. First, it has not advanced the industrial development of Africa in any significant way. The continent remains the least industrialized in the world. In 1980 for instance, relative to world manufacturing output, Africa's share of manufacturing value was only 0.9 per cent as compared with 2.7 per cent and 6.0 per cent for South and East Asia and Latin America, respectively - and there is no reason to believe that it has increased since then. However, as we have noted already, the major and perhaps the sole positive consequence of the import substitution industrial strategy has been the establishment of a clearly definable modern manufacturing sector distinguished by its use of modern machinery. The scale and size of this sector varies from country to country, but these industrial establishments are plagued generally by inefficiency and low productivity. The underlying assumption here is that this situation could be remedied with a more efficient use of labour - and in this respect we could learn a great deal from the experiences of other developing countries, especially in Asia, which have successfully progressed beyond import substitution to the large-scale export of manufactured goods. Highly efficient management and high labour commitment and productivity have played a major role in this development.

Wage Employment in West Africa

A successful industrialization process depends on several factors, both human and non-human. The human factors are the entrepreneurial skills available in society, management expertise and workers. We are concerned here with the latter category - industrial workers. Like industrialization, wage employment is a recent phenomenon in West Africa, and, as in the rest of the continent, a consequence of colonial capitalist activities. This implies that prior to colonialism no West Africans sold their labour in return for remuneration of any kind. Work that was important to traditional African societies was done primarily for subsistence or to fulfil certain customary obligations, but never for payment. In a traditional African setting, labour was not a commodity to be bought and sold on the market, but an obligation that one owed as a member of a household and kinship unit. Precapitalist relations of production involved the allocation of labour to specific tasks on the basis of sex and age. Women undertook certain domestic and farming duties until they became too old to work. Men were assigned tasks not on the basis of capital, skills or strength (as in capitalist society), but on the basis of age. However, the introduction of western capitalist economic activities changed the old ways of work. According to Karl Marx (1906):

> Capitalist production only really begins. . .when each individual capitalist employs simultaneously a comparatively large number of labourers, when consequently the labour process is carried out on an extensive scale and yields relatively large quantities of products. A greater number of labourers working together at the same time, in one place (or if you will, in the same field of labour) in order to produce the same sort of commodities under the mastership of one capitalist constitutes, both historically and logically, the starting-point of capitalist production.

The system that developed in the early years of colonization in Africa cannot strictly be called capitalism *per se*, and the term 'mercantilist capitalism' has been suggested to explain the phenomenon. However, just as in other societies, this system created a labour market in West Africa, and required the services of a large number of labourers to service the European trading companies and various colonial administrative departments. During the initial period of colonization, however, approximately between 1880 and 1930, colonial employers experienced considerable difficulties in recruiting enough African labour to service these emergent economic and administrative activities. Why was there a severe shortage of wage labour and how was it overcome? W. A. Lewis's (1954) two-sector model of labour allocation, which postulated a movement of labour from a low-income 'subsistence sector', offers an inadequate explanation of the situation. Under normal circumstances, one would expect people to leave the rural subsistence sector for the capitalist sector where the wage rate is some 30 to 50 per cent higher. Since productivity in the capitalist sector is postulated to be sufficiently high to make the payment of higher wage rates consistent with the rate of profit that employers expect in order to undertake production, the capitalist sector was said to enjoy 'unlimited' supplies of labour in the sense that at that level of wages, practically everyone in the subsistence sector would be prepared to enter wage employment. However, this did not happen in West Africa, partly because the wage rate was kept as low as possible. This was a deliberate colonial policy based on the belief that high wages would be ineffectual, if not counter-productive. Colonialists tended to ascribe the reluctance of Africans to enter (and remain in) employment to 'economic irrationality': in as much as Africans worked only to earn a set sum of money and generally put leisure before work (they were considered 'indolent') raising wages would merely encourage Africans to leave their jobs even sooner. This was the infamous theory of the backward-sloping labour supply function. If Africans were paid a very low wage it would take a longer period of time to achieve the target - hence the almost starvation wages paid to early wage-workers. According to Arrighi (1968):

> Market mechanisms were largely discarded in the determination of wages and the real wage rate came to be customarily fixed at the level that would provide for the subsistence of a *single* worker while working in the capitalist sector and a small margin to meet the more urgent cash income requirements of his family (which continues to reside in the peasant sector).

In addition to low wages, there were very poor housing arrangements in the emerging urban centres and sometimes quite appalling working conditions. Berg (1965) argued that:

> It is unreasonable to expect that men would willingly expose themselves to the wage-earning experience in these circumstances; that they would trade the certainty and security of village life for the discomforts of working outside for money. The wonder is not that the Africans in the beginning showed little enthusiasm for paid employment and the money income that would be earned. The real wonder is that there were as many volunteers as there were.

Life in the rural villages was not only secure and predictable but there was also alternative employment. Unlike Europe, where capitalism created a working class by destroying the existing means of subsistence, in Africa the traditional economy was left largely intact to produce raw materials for metropolitan industries. Thus an individual might decide to stay entirely in the rural sector - as many people did - and produce crops (cash or food) or engage in some village craft or 'cottage industry' such as cloth-weaving. In West Africa 'Land was abundant relative to the number of Africans who lived on it, and rural misery of the harshness that was common in some Middle-Eastern or Asian countries was rarely encountered in Africa.' Similarly, the long journeys through hostile territories that were necessary to reach the urban centres, as well as fear of sickness and death in an alien environment, were factors that deterred many Africans from leaving their villages. The combination of all these factors meant an acute labour shortage during the early years of colonization. For most Africans during that period, the cost of taking up wage employment far outweighed the rewards they might obtain from it. Consequently, many of them remained in their villages or made short trips to earn enough money to meet social obligations. Labour shortages worsened with the expansion of colonialism, and the need for labour - especially unskilled labour for the mines, plantations, railway, roads, and so on - became urgent. In an attempt to rectify the situation a number of 'political' mechanisms were adopted that were intended to expand the supply of labour so that it matched demand. One of the most important of these mechanisms was the rapid monetarization of traditional economies. By monetarization we mean the pervasiveness of money as a medium of exchange in the economy at large; the development of the attributes of what we now call the modern monetary system, including the credit system. This involved the introduction of European monetary forms that were made the sole means of exchange and by which manufactured commodities could be purchased, and was accompanied by the imposition of taxes that had to be paid with European money. Similarly, the monetarization process had the consequence of gradually converting traditional and customary obligations, which had been met in the past through other avenues, into money payments. Even with all these mechanisms in place, there were still labour shortages. As the pace of colonization quickened throughout West Africa, more labour was required to service the needs of the various administrative departments and European industry, and more direct measures were taken to provide it. The use of force as a means to compel Africans to take up wage employment was introduced in both the French and British colonies on the West Coast. Lord Lugard, a strong exponent of the use of forced labour, argued that 'Among the primitive tribes a measure of compulsion through their tribal chiefs in order to obtain labour for railway construction and other important works is justifiable as our educative policy to remove fear and suspicion.'

The various measures adopted by the colonial authorities combined to leave many Africans with no choice but to migrate to the urban areas in search of wage employment. However, this new form of employment was regarded as temporary. As soon as the worker obtained enough money to fulfil obligations or buy desired items, both job and urban centre were abandoned for the rural base. This was the definition of the famous African 'target worker' who worked only as long as it took to achieve a target. Once this was achieved there was no longer an incentive to remain in town. Thus a continuous circulation of workers from the villages to the towns moved from agricultural employment into urban wage employment. This circular movement has been one cause of the low productivity that has characterized both sectors.

Labour shortages effectively ended in the early 1930s, by which time many Africans had become acquainted with wage employment and the urban way of life that it entailed. Gradually more people came to the towns in search of jobs. This proletarianization process was assisted to a significant degree by the 1930s world economic recession, the Great Depression. The prices of primary products, which formed the economic mainstay of the colonies, collapsed, forcing many Africans, who had hitherto depended on agriculture for their subsistence, to migrate to the towns in search of alternative employment. In the towns, employment opportunities shrank as economic activities declined drastically. With more people entering urban centres in the face of diminishing employment opportunities, there were more applicants than jobs for the first time in West Africa, i.e., unemployment became a reality, at least at the lower strata of wage employment. However, there was one positive outcome from this state of affairs - the urban wage-labour force in most West African towns became stabilized. This is not to imply that labour became stationary - in fact there was a great deal of labour mobility as people moved from 'saturated' areas to those locations where opportunities still existed. Rather, stabilization of labour implies the emergence of a type of worker who looked primarily, if not exclusively, to wage-earning for individual and family support and was prepared to face the change in lifestyle that this demanded. As labour becomes stabilized workers tend to adopt permanent long-term residence under urban conditions - and the growth of urbanization is thus a rough measure of a stable form of labour. West African towns and cities grew rapidly during the 1930s, so that by the eve of

World War II a more or less permanent and stabilized wage-labour force had emerged throughout much of the region. Cohen (1976) suggested some other equally important factors that advanced the process of stabilization very significantly. First, production in the rural areas shifted slowly out of the hands of the community into individual peasant proprietorship. This had the effect of displacing a number of people whose claim to land had been based formerly on communal ownership. Cohen points out, however, that this process is still far from complete in much of Africa. Secondly, employment opportunities in the cities opened up as industry and administration expanded. Even though these opportunities were rarely sufficient to meet the demand for jobs, social aspirations (which derived partly from the expansion of education) remained high, and many unemployed workers preferred to remain in the towns. Finally, Cohen noted that the degree of impoverishment that became common in many African rural economies meant that a return to the land was in any case unfeasible for most migrants. For many of the newly urbanized Africans who could not take up wage employment, either from choice or because there were no jobs available, the sole option was to engage in small-scale informal-sector economic activities, which still characterize West African urban centres today. These activities included petty trading, photography, carpentry, tailoring, and so on. During the war years the numbers of urban wage workers increased further as a result of increased military and economic activities. 'The expansion of production, the establishment of new local industries and the various military constructions involved a growing number of workers and employees, thereby inflating the urban population' (Sik, 1974). After the war, this process continued until well into the 1970s in many West African countries.

The rural villages perform vital social welfare functions for urban dwellers in times of crisis. Although many Africans now reside permanently in towns and cities, only a very small minority sever their connections with their villages completely. For many Africans these villages remain the last resort in times of exceptional stress or difficulty, such as prolonged unemployment or illness. Many workers (and urban dwellers in general) continue to fulfil their traditional obligations, partly to ensure the goodwill and co-operation of kin, safeguard their rights to land and establish an honoured place for themselves in local society.

The reluctance of most Africans to sever links with the rural areas has been interpreted by a number of western scholars as evidence that African workers are still basically target workers even though the target has changed from 'particular objects like bicycles or particular sums of money' to the search for 'the attainment of a permanently higher standard of life'. This is seen as one important reason for the low productivity of African workers.

Overall, then, the argument is that in precolonial West Africa, work was not performed for remuneration, a system that was introduced by colonialism. While there were labour shortages initially as Africans refused to embrace wage employment for a variety of logical and valid reasons, this situation was overcome by the 1930s, when urbanization had established momentum. More migrants entered the towns than there were jobs available. Finally, a stabilized wage labour force, committed to industrialism and urbanism, emerged throughout the region. Much of the existing literature suggests that this industrial labour force compares unfavourably with those in other continents - and the next section accordingly looks briefly at views of Africans as industrial workers.

African Labour Productivity

Having argued that both industrialization and wage employment are relatively recent phenomena in West Africa, and that hard work is a valued norm in traditional societies, we will look at how Africans have fared as industrial workers. How have social scientists and others regarded their performance? Unfortunately the predominant opinion is that African labour is largely inefficient - a notion that has persisted from colonial times to the present. Most writings on African industry present African workers as low producers compared with workers in other parts of the world.

> One does not exaggerate by stating that there already exists a clearly definable, unique and fully elaborated construction of the African worker. The universality of the image is so great, both in and out of economic literature, as to rank it as a major tenet in the folklore of modern Africa. . . .The source material for this picture of the African worker is a number of Government reports and individual studies. These studies have depicted a situation of excessively high rates of absenteeism and turnover - lack of punctuality and inefficiency and inaptitude in the workplace. (Kilby, 1961)

The review of the literature intended here looks at selected source material and examines the reasons that have been advanced to explain the alleged inefficiency of African labour. Comparatively few studies have opposed this generalized view of African workers, noting like Gluckman (1961) that 'An African townsman is a townsman' and 'An African miner is a miner' - and a sample of these viewpoints will also be outlined here.

Historically, the measurement and evaluation of African labour productivity began during the early colonial period at a time when Africans were regarded as culturally and physically inferior to Europeans. This was a common point of agreement among early European managers, social scientists and commentators. De Briey's (1955) argument is typical:

> If the output of unskilled labour in industry here were to be taken as a yardstick, the picture of the African worker's standards of productivity would undoubtedly be gloomy. It is unanimously recognised that the output of unskilled Afri-

> can workers is extremely low in almost all the undertakings that employ them.

De Briey went on to provide several illustrative studies in attempts to buttress his argument: first, an attempt to measure the productivity of labour in a factory in Durban (Union of South Africa) showed that the output of the average unskilled migrant worker was only 29 per cent of the figure taken to be optimum. Secondly, an inquiry held in Douala (French-administered Cameroon) found that:

> As compared with a white worker's output, that [of] a Negro varies between one-third and one-seventh or one-eighth depending on the employer and the trade (or within a trade). The usual proportion is about one quarter. In other words, it takes a Negro four days to do what a white man does in one.

From these examples it would appear that physically and perhaps mentally African workers were inferior to their white counterparts - hence the inability of Africans to compete or produce as much as white workers. However, few scholars subscribed to this notion. As the International Labour Organization stated in its *African Labour Survey* (1958):

> What has emerged is that, while it is accepted that there is no scientific basis for the proposition that any initial incapacity in the African rests on any difference in hereditary biological constitution between him and members of any other racial group, it is a fact that *by tradition and background* the African is singularly ill-adapted for assimilation as an effective element in a wage economy on the modern pattern, that *the reason that leads him to seek paid wage labour* heavily influences his attitude to work and his response to incentives and that his reactions differ widely from those of the European worker, whose background and aims are so different. (Emphasis added)

Thus, while repudiating that any inherent biological disability was responsible for the inefficiency of African labour, the ILO survey emphasizes two factors that require further elaboration. These are the traditional values of Africans and the reasons that led Africans into wage employment initially. In the literature, African cultures and background are usually regarded as the antithesis of that which exists in western societies. This is perhaps best illustrated by reference to the patterns that are used to characterize African traditional societies: affectivity, collectivism, particularism, ascription and diffuseness of roles. Western industrial society is characterized by effective neutrality, individualism, universalism, achievement and role specificity. Coming from African traditional backgrounds therefore, the worker is hard put to adapt to the novel demands of the industrial way of life. The maladjustment of many Africans thus results in poor performance at their industrial duties. Dawson (1963) argued, in his article on the Temne and Mende of Sierra Leone, that traditional values allowed them to work with an industrial organization, but that 'The degree of efficiency they have attained is limited by the secondary role which work values have played in traditional Temne Society.' According to him, members of the Temne Poro and Mende Wunde have traditionally exercised authority and held values oriented towards war rather than work, and they have not been able to adapt to this new industrial role. Nevertheless, he cautioned that:

> The main characteristic of these groups with low assessed work performance in the mine is, however, an emphasis on traditional values, which emphasis has not been modified by contact with such urban processes as education and industrial training. The strong relationship demonstrated between work performance and traditional values does therefore appear to explain why such high correlations were obtained between the traditional versus Western Concept Formation scale and ratings of work performance. (Ibid.)

The implication here is that the more Africans are exposed to urbanism and western cultural influences, and the less the influence of traditional values, the higher or better the job performance. However, as we will see, this clearly has not been the case.

The second factor involves those elements that compel Africans to seek wage employment. Again, as the *African Labour Survey* quotation showed, there is some consensus that the factors that drive Africans to wage employment differ from those that influence European workers. One dominant explanation in the literature is the general belief that Africans are not 'natural' urban workers, but permanent migrants, and in fact this was a widely accepted explanation for all failings of African labourers. Soper, for instance, states categorically that 'Migrancy is at the heart of the productivity problem.'

> Labour migration considerably reduces African efficiency in industry, for on entering or re-entering wage employment [the African worker] takes some time to get accustomed to the new routine and with the high labour turnover, he tends to leave just as he is getting settled. (1958)

Again, the reason for this constant movement between urban wage employment and rural (agricultural) employment is that Africans are simply target workers. Unfortunately this view persists to the present. Many western managers and social scientists still regard African workers as not being totally committed to wage employment. As Elkan (1960) suggested:

> These days there are few target workers of this kind (i.e., those who 'work only long enough to acquire the cash needed to buy those things which only cash can buy, and when they have earned enough they leave employment and return to subsistence farms') and most Africans only too plainly aspire to a higher standard of life - though one would

> therefore have to dismiss the whole concept of the target worker. If we define targets not in terms of particular objects like bicycles or particular sums of money, but more generally, as means to attaining a permanently higher standard of life, the concept is still useful and can indeed serve to throw light on the reasons why people engage in employment only temporarily.

This is a very curious argument, for if targets are defined as 'higher standards of life', the concept would apply to European or American workers as well: the basic goal of workers worldwide is to be able to afford a higher standard of living. It is not peculiar to Africans alone.

Other reasons have been given to explain African job performance. J. Guilbot (1956) suggested, on the basis of a study in Douala, Cameroon, that the major determinants of the poor productivity of Africans are:

1 high alcohol consumption;
2 lack of adequate supervision.

The supervision factor has been a recurrent theme, both among early writers and in contemporary studies. Major Orde-Brown (1933) argued that 'The outstanding disadvantage of African labour is the necessity for constant supervision if an adequate output is to be secured and this usually entails considerable expense.' The implication here is obvious - Africans are 'generally incapable of assuming responsibility and must be closely supervised for the best achievement'. This view is still current in Africa and many managers, both foreign and indigenous, subscribe to it. However, Orde-Brown suggested further that what was wrong was the existence, in the minds of both African workers and European employers, of the slavery mentality. According to him, 'When slavery was abolished, the African ceased to be an effective worker.' He argued that 'Freed slaves generally proved irresponsible, were reluctant to work hard unless closely supervised and, no longer having a universal provider, they tended to sink lower and lower into social squalor.'

Other writers have followed a direction similar to Orde-Brown's. In a study of the African town of Leopoldville, E. Capelle (1956) investigated frequent complaints by employers about the low output of workers. He suggested that the reason was 'a lack of any desire to improve their situation on the part of Africans'. Similarly, Dr C. H. Northcott conducted the 'African Labour Efficiency Survey' and concluded that 'The beginning and end of the problem of efficiency is the individual African, often a man who has not acquired the habit of disciplined work, to whom physical effort is a thing to be avoided, and who has not learned that in a wage economy there is a correlation between wage and effort.'

Much of the literature could be dismissed as jaundiced and the product of a lack of knowledge of labour history. Nevertheless, other writers, even during the colonial era, saw the problem of low productivity in a different light. They saw it not as the result of any inherent characteristic of Africans but rather as the result of external factors, among which they frequently cited poor management and discriminatory practices. Elkan (1956), for example, shows how faulty recruitment practices could be responsible for putting the wrong people on the job. He gives the example of how men are picked from a crowd assembled outside the gates of the industrial establishment on the first day of the month, presumably according to the impression created by their appearance. The result of such a method is that 'Men are frequently placed in jobs which they dislike or at which they are incompetent, and being new in the factory they leave sooner than ask to be transferred to other work.'

Related to the problem of 'poor management' are the appalling conditions under which Africans live and work. This was particularly so in the early days of industrial development in Africa. Gussman (1953) summarized the situation thus:

> The average urban African is unhealthy, badly housed, uneducated, and he lacks any security in town even if he happens to have been born there. These are his greatest and constant worries. The fact that he cannot afford a shilling for a drink or beer worries him as little proportionately as it does the average European. Neither money nor the work that he performs can release him from any of his real troubles. He cannot obtain better health, a better education for himself or his children, or a better or permanent home in the urban areas.

Although written more than three decades ago, these comments are still highly relevant to the situation in present-day Africa. Because of the poor social conditions in the cities, many African workers suffer from a wide range of diseases. Doucy (1956) observed the physical conditions of workers in Belgian Congo:

1 They all suffer from parasitic worms of the intestine;
2 some suffer from parasitic worms of the blood;
3 all have malaria;
4 all have incipient yaws, for which they have received little or no treatment;
5 most have or have had gonorrhoea;
6 many have syphilis.
7 Some of these conditions reduce their haemoglobin level, which in many cases is as low as 65%, i.e., a red blood count of 3-3.5 million.

Allowing for exaggeration, it would be unreasonable to expect maximum performance from workers who are ill-fed and prone to the diseases described above. Similarly, conditions of work affect productivity. Workers who labour under appalling conditions cannot perform efficiently. Kilby

(1961) concluded that indirect measures, i.e., absenteeism and turnover 'clearly indicate that the African's performance as a wage-earner is satisfactory and can by no means be construed to suggest that the worker is unstable and restless and prone to absent himself apparently without valid reason'. It is also evident that the degree of absenteeism and turnover is a fairly accurate measure, not of the acculturation of African workers, but of the wages paid, conditions of service and the physical surroundings.

More contemporary studies have also echoed these sentiments, and for the most part many of the earlier explanations and rationalizations have been abandoned. There is at present a consensus that the African has emerged as an 'industrial man' [*sic.*], fully committed to the industrial way of life - and one of the major ingredients of commitment to the industrial way of life is long-term urban residence. As Gutkind (1968) argued:

> A commitment to, and an involvement in, urbanism as a way of life might be viewed as an important prerequisite for effective participation, and an understanding of the demands of urban wage labour: this is to say stability of employment, and the willingness to accept and abide by the demands made by new occupations and production processes are related to the degree of involvement in, and acceptance of urbanism as a way of life.

Evidence shows that most African workers have fully accepted permanent urban residence. This is not to imply that they have broken links totally with their rural origins. They still make visits to rural villages, especially for cultural and traditional ceremonies, but their commitment is to urban residence. As a large-scale urban survey in Tanzania showed:

> Towns are no longer merely employment centres where a peasant goes for short periods to supplement his income. The urban labour force is now a modern labour force in the

> sense that its commitment to wage employment is not shared with a commitment to agricultural self-employment. Increasing stability has gone hand in hand with the increasing acquisition of skills, the acceptance of industrial discipline and specialization, resulting in a large part from the accumulation of experience and on-the-job training. And the towns are no longer mere dormitories for transient workers but now function as the locus of activity of a growing urban community.

Notwithstanding the positive factor of urbanism and African adaptation to its mode of life, reports of poor productivity have persisted. The World Bank, in its 1981 report on Africa, argued that:

> African labour tends to compare unfavourably with many other parts of the world. A comparison of six African and four South American textile mills financed by the IFC showed that the average number of spinners per 1,000 spindle shifts and the average number of weavers per equivalent loom shift was more than twice as high in Africa.

The Bank attributes this low productivity to Africa's early stage of industrial development, a situation that the Bank suggests would improve with time and as industrialization progresses on the continent.

More recently, a great deal of blame for Africa's low productivity has been attributed to other job-related factors and not to any inherent incapabilities or attitudes of the workers. As Kilby (1961) suggested 'Low labour productivity cannot be attributed to the attitudes and capabilities of the African worker. On the contrary, where low levels of output prevail, the burden must fall on those responsible for management and supervision of the enterprise.' This is a point that Onyemelukwe (1966) fully agrees with, and argues that a solution to the problem is to bring management as near as possible to the shop-floor workers. Ogunbameru (1984) studied two factories in Ondo State, Nigeria and found that workers cited consistent machine breakdown as a result of poor maintenance as the major factor responsible for low performance. Other factors cited, in order of importance, were poor and irregular wages, poor environmental conditions, lack of skills and bad supervisory style, and the work group.

One basic point remains: in contemporary Africa, labour productivity is considered low compared with other parts of the world. Various reasons have been advanced to explain the situation, yet scant progress has been made in resolving it. If, as some studies have argued, there is nothing inherently wrong with African workers, then the solution must be sought in the mechanisms for motivating the worker at work. The next chapter looks at the socio-economic background of workers, as this largely determines orientation to work.

Notes

[1] The leading manufacturing industries in the 1970s were as follows: in Ghana food processing contributed 13.5% of gross manufacturing output in 1976, textiles 12.5%, beverages 11.6%, wood and petroleum products 9.4% each, and clothing 4.4%. In Côte d'Ivoire in 1978 chemicals and fats contributed 17.6%, food and tobacco 16.1%, textiles 13.7%, metal 11%, and lumber 7.3% of total manufacturing output. Nigeria's manufacturing base was more diversified, with textiles accounting for 13.8% of total in 1974, food and tobacco 10.8%, brewing 7.2%, soap, perfume and cosmetics 6.5%, fabricated metal products and grain mill products 4.2% each, structural metal products 3.9%, basic metal, cutlery and tools 3.7%, vegetable oil 3.3%, motor vehicle assembly 3.1%, printing 2.8%, and cement, lime and plaster 2.6%.

5 Socio-Economic Background

In the previous chapter it was argued that workers' orientation to work is a key variable in explaining their behaviour at work. What is the source of these orientations? Goldthorpe *et al.* (1968) suggested that they arise from outside the workplace - from workers' social experiences and relationships. These social experiences and relationships derive in turn from the structure of the prevalent socio-economic order - orientation to work cannot arise independently of this structure. In other words, the motivation to enter into formal employment is a function of the total social and economic situation in which the worker is immersed and by which personal aspirations are crystallized. An analysis of the socio-economic context is thus a vital step toward an adequate understanding of work-related behaviour:

> The attitudes which men hold towards work are a reflection of a complex set of inter-related values which exist in each culture. . . .Work motivation requires appraisal within its social context. It should not be regarded as an isolated activity which may be transposed from one group to another without taking account of the customary attitudes of both groups to this facet of their culture. (Glass, 1961)

More than anything else, the economic structure of society determines the total social situation:

> Once we understand what the material assets and constraints of a society are, how the society produces goods to meet its material needs, how the goods are distributed and what types of social relations arise from the organization of production, we have come a long way to understanding the culture of that society, its laws, its religious system, its political system and even its mode of thought. (Ake, 1981)

This is not to imply that a society's economic system is wholly independent. Although Marxist scholars regard it as the dominant system, it is influenced by others - political systems, for example - which exert multiple and powerful influences upon it. All things considered, however, it is the *mode of production* of material goods that underlies other social systems, and this must be a prominent feature of any analysis of the attitudes and behaviour of individuals within that society.

West African countries were formerly colonies of European powers and are now undergoing changes to their basic institutions and values, in which 'traditional' African subsistence societies are gradually giving way under the forces of modernization. The consequent social, economic and, at times, political changes have become increasingly painful to these countries. Economic development has taken place at a much slower pace than the acquisition of new aspirations and expectations as a result of expanding educational opportunities - in fact, poverty has become an everyday reality for the majority of West African citizens. This must be considered a key factor in any discussion of the 'total social situation'. This background of deprivation and poverty is largely resonsible for moulding and subsequently modifying workers' orientations, aspirations and expectations - and their awareness of national economic changes is intensified by residence in urban centres. The economies of developing countries fluctuate a great deal, as they are virtually dependent on the economies of the developed countries; in fact, their subordinate position in the metropolis-satellite matrix makes industrial development impossible. (An economy is dependent to the extent that its international relations and the articulation of its internal structure make it incapable of autocentric development.) Now we will look briefly at the prevailing economic conditions of the three countries represented here.

Prevailing Economic Conditions

Côte d'Ivoire

Until recently, Côte d'Ivoire was widely regarded as an economic miracle in Africa and evidence of successful capitalist development on a backward continent. An agricultural country depending mainly on two cash crops, cocoa and coffee, for its export revenue, Côte d'Ivoire experienced steady growth throughout the 1960s and 1970s, when the industrial sector grew at a staggering 15 per cent of GDP. With a relatively small population and a growing economy, Côte d'Ivoire relied on migrant labour from neighbouring countries, and today it is estimated that foreigners make up over one fifth of the total population. However, serious crises were triggered when declining receipts from traditional coffee and cocoa exports coincided with external debt-servicing obligations that amounted to over 30 per cent of export goods and services. In 1984 the national debt reached CFA 2,167 billion or 74.1 per cent of GDP, and debt-servicing amounted to 28 per cent of exports of goods and services. The government was forced to take corrective measures, which included the closure of a number of unprofitable government establishments and curtailing government investment expenditure. The popular consensus was that an economic reversal lay ahead, but this has not materialized. According to one informed source 'Officials (of the World Bank) responsible for the Ivorian case are alarmed by the difficulties the country is facing in managing its readjustment.' The optimism shown by the authors of the 1986

World Bank memorandum on Côte d'Ivoire now looks extremely ill-founded. The manufacturing sector, whose revival was anticipated by Bank officials in 1986, is on the point of collapse. This can be considered a particular embarrassment in light of the World Bank's insistence on a 40 per cent reduction in Ivorian tariff barriers, a decision that has turned out to be disastrous as Ivorian chemical, textile, shoe and automobile assembly industries crumble in the face of international competition.

The consequences of the economic down-turn have been especially severe for the average citizen. A sharp rise in inflation led to an exorbitant increase in the cost of living and to increased unemployment. In the manufacturing industries, employment fell from 71,373 in 1980 to 68,359 in 1982 and to only 60,359 in 1984. At the same time wages and salaries were frozen as part of the readjustment programme: between 1982 and 1985 the minimum hourly industrial wage remained static at CFA 191.40. Sandbrook (1982), in a sample survey of 1,000 manual workers in urban food-processing plants, sought to expose the roots of the low productivity and high rate of absenteeism among the predominantly immigrant workers from surrounding countries. The most important factor was found to be general physical debility among these workers, a consequence of nutritional deficiencies, the prevalence of parasitic and endemic diseases, and alcoholism. There is today a current and widespread psychological malaise associated with a sense of hopelessness and alienation from work - a situation that is bound to worsen with a declining economy and increasing unemployment. However, adverse conditions in the capital Abidjan have not stemmed migration from the rural areas or from neighbouring countries where conditions are even worse. Abidjan has an estimated population of 2 million and is still growing. Between 1955 and 1975, the city's population grew by about 10.2 per cent p.a.: if this growth rate is sustained the population can be expected to double by the end of the century. One interesting feature of Abidjan is the fact that, in spite of rising unemployment, a large number of foreigners still have jobs. This situation has been attributed to the preference among indigenous Ivorians for white-collar or Civil Service jobs, leaving manual and factory jobs to foreigners, mainly from Mali and Burkina Faso, and increasingly from Ghana. Unless the economy revives, increasing numbers of Ivorians will be forced to take manual or factory jobs, and some have already done so. Consumer price indices from 1980 to 1985 indicate that government austerity measures may be having a beneficial effect on the economy, as inflation has decreased significantly.

Ghana

While Côte d'Ivoire has recently suffered an economic downturn, the situation in Ghana has been much worse. Between 1960 and 1970, Ghana's GDP grew by a modest 2.1 per cent, but between 1970 and 1979, it declined markedly, recording a depressing -0.1 per cent growth. Since the late 1960s, the country has been in steady economic decline, 'bringing Ghana from [being] probably the most prosperous of the West African colonies to a low point in 1983 when hunger was widespread, even in the capital Accra'. In the same year the official cost of living index rose by 122 per cent. The following figures indicate the desperate state of the Ghanaian economy: between 1970 and 1980 agricultural and industrial production fell by 1.2% p.a., income per caput fell by 3.1% p.a. (representing a one-third drop in real income over the decade), and the volume of exports by 8.4 % p.a. While worker output declined by 1.7% p.a., and the real wage rate by 13.4% p.a., the average rate of inflation over the decade was 34.8%. Between 1979 and 1982, GDP fell by an average of 6.1% p.a.

According to the World Bank, few countries in the world have suffered such a rapid decline as Ghana during the period in question. Most significant for us is the fact that the burden of declining incomes has fallen disproportionately on cocoa farmers, producers of goods and commodities, and urban fixed-salary and wage earners. Food availability per caput in 1982 was estimated to be 30 per cent lower than it had been ten years previously. The decline in income per caput has had predictable consequences - an increase in the incidence of absolute poverty, growing unemployment, flourishing illegal activities (especially the growth of parallel-marketeering) and the migration of thousands of young Ghanaians to all parts of the world.

The government has introduced a restructuring and readjustment programme and has taken out an IMF loan under the usual conditions. The newsletter *Africa Confidential* notes (in connection with the loan), that:

> The national currency, the Cedi, was devalued from 2.75 Cedis to the US dollar in September 1983 to the present 162 Cedis to the US dollar fixed at a weekly auction. Other austerity measures proposed by the IMF and accepted by the government have included the removal of subsidies on health, education and other social services. The price of petrol has increased from C12.30 a gallon to the present C195 a gallon. In 1981 Rawlings expressed disgust that the price of a chicken was C70. A chicken now costs over C700. To soften the blow to workers, salaries have been increased but only to a minimum level of C112.

Some agencies, including the World Bank, have predicted an improvement in the country's economic prospects, yet these are still to be felt among the poorer strata of society. Sandbrook (1984) reports an early study conducted by the Ghana Ministry of Health in 1971, which discovered that, although an average 69 per cent of worker's take-home pay was spent on food purchases, many workers in Accra complained that they frequently had to rely upon kolanuts to dull their hunger pains after the middle of the month. There is no reason to believe that the situation has changed significantly since then.

Nigeria

Nigeria is the most populous and potentially one of the richest countries in Africa. At independence in 1960 it had a strong agricultural economy relying on cocoa, groundnuts, palm produce, cotton, and other agricultural commodities for export earnings. On the basis of its agricultural exports Nigeria enjoyed modest economic growth throughout the decade. However, the discovery and commercial exploitation of crude oil changed things dramatically. Increased earnings from petroleum exports prompted high levels of real economic growth and by the mid-1970s Nigeria ranked as the dominant economy in sub-Saharan Africa, and was the continent's major petroleum exporter. The tremendous increase in revenue derived from oil exports enabled the government to embark on a very ambitious capitalist development programme with substantial investment in infrastructure, education, social services and industrial development. This development programme, however, resulted in a crucial dysfunction - the agricultural sector was left to stagnate, farms became unprofitable and many rural people were forced to leave them in pursuit of urban employment and contracts. By 1985 agriculture contributed to less than 3 per cent of total exports.

By the late 1970s, however, the oil bubble began to deflate as world oil prices fell. By 1981 the oil boom had finally collapsed and 'The government found itself financially overextended, with insufficient revenue from petroleum to meet the growing import bill or to finance important projects.' Since 1981, the country's GDP has continued to decline - by slightly more than 5 per cent in 1981, by 3.4 per cent in 1982, 4.4 per cent in 1983 and by only 1 per cent in 1984 (a recovery that can be attributed to improvements in oil prices). This can be compared to the period between 1975 and 1980 when the GDP growth rate in real terms was an average of 0.6-0.7 per cent p.a. By 1986, GDP was only 0.7 per cent higher in real terms than it had been in 1973. The population growth rate, estimated at 3.2 per cent, has not helped matters. Faced with popular disapproval at home, the government refused to take out an IMF loan, but introduced a Structural Adjustment Programme (SAP), which some commentators have considered harsher than IMF conditions. Elements of the adjustment programme include a 'back-door' devaluation of the national currency (the naira), removal of substantial subsidies from petroleum products, an across-the-board wage cut, and so on. The consequences have been severe for the majority of citizens and the cost of living has risen steadily (there was an average 5.5 per cent increase in the cost of all consumer items in 1984/85).

The steady rise in inflation and the cost of living was accompanied by large-scale job losses. All sectors of the economy, and especially industry and construction, have been affected by the economic slow-down and forced to cut staff. According to the Nigerian Manufacturing Association, about 200,000 employees (approximately 40 per cent of the industrial labour force) are estimated to have been retrenched between 1984 and 1986. The general social and economic atmosphere of the country is conveyed by a 1981 ILO study:

> Probably more people are living in poverty than before the oil boom started. . . .The wages of those in regular employment buy no more in relation to the cost of living than they did in the mid-1960s. . .[there is] chronic and possibly increasing ill-health, with a continuing heavy incidence of diseases of poverty. . .semi-stagnation in the rural economy causes heavy migration to the towns and cities.

The situation outlined above applies to much of West Africa. The 1980s has been an unfortunate decade for these economies, partly for reasons beyond their control, which include drought and the collapse of the world market for agricultural products. However, we are concerned with the consequences of economic problems for people at large, and especially the poorer sectors of the population. We have seen that one major consequence - the increase in rural-urban migration - has continued even during periods of serious unemployment in the urban centres. Todaro's (1973) explanation for this phenomenon is still valid. He argued that the key to an understanding of the seemingly paradoxical phenomenon of continued migration to centres of high unemployment lies in viewing the migration process from an 'expected' or permanent income approach. Expected income relates not only to the actual wage paid to an urban worker, but also to the probability of success in securing wage employment in any given period. It is the combination and interaction of these two variables - the urban-rural real income differential and the probability of securing an urban job - that determine the rate and magnitude of rural-urban migration in tropical Africa. Migrants believe that once they arrive in an urban centre, it is only a matter of time before they secure a job. Having convinced themselves of this probability, they are prepared to settle down and wait, swelling the ranks of 'the reserve army of the unemployed'. For these migrants, the aspirations and expectations they bring with them are reinforced or modified by their experiences of the urban way of life. Similarly, the aspirations and expectations of people born or raised in the cities are shaped by prevalent urban norms and values. Nevertheless, traditional cultural and social values do not simply disappear - far from it, they persist with surprising tenacity. Rather than encouraging the migrant to shed traditional customs, orientations and behaviour patterns, urbanism merely modifies them.

The hardening of class boundaries in urban centres is an important consequence of this set of economic circumstances, and certain broad class categories can be identified by even the most casual observer. The simple dichotomy between 'rich' and 'poor', although useful, does not permit a graphic description of the current West African situation, as more complex social structures have emerged in the three countries studied. While it is possible to identify similar classes in Nigeria, Côte d'Ivoire and Ghana, there are subtle differences that will be pointed out later.

At the apex of the social structure are the ruling classes, composed of several different groups: first, there is the political class, which is composed of politicians (in Côte d'Ivoire), and military rulers (in Nigeria and Ghana). Secondly, there are corporate interests, or the business class, which is closely allied with and sometimes indistinguishable from the political class. In Côte d'Ivoire this class consists primarily of the owners of large plantations, a phenomenon that is also emerging slowly in Nigeria. The final category making up the ruling class consists of people in the top echelons of the Civil Service, the military (where they are not in power), the police services and the judiciary. These groups are all made up of individuals whose proximity to state power enables them to accumulate substantial economic interests.

Directly below the ruling class is a larger, though diminishing, middle class, whose members belong mostly to the professions - law, medicine, teaching, the private and public sectors of employment and the middle level of the armed services. This class is distinguished from the others by two main factors: it is made up mostly of educated individuals and most of them are employees. The owners of small-scale businesses, who usually live among the urban masses, are included here as well. In terms of income, this group qualifies as middle class, although individuals within it usually identify themselves as part of the urban poor, among whom they live and to whom they serve as a reference group. Below the middle class is the largest class, the urban poor, whose composition we shall discuss in due course.

The delineation into classes attempted above is only useful for analytical purposes, and in real life the demarcation lines differentiating one class from another have yet to be clarified. Nevertheless, they have crystallized sufficiently to be visible at least in the capital cities of West Africa, although here too certain factors distort the emerging picture. These West African cities are structured in a manner that encourages the persistence of what has been referred to as a 'rural orientation'. As Lloyd (1967) noted, West African towns cannot be divided easily into compact territorial subunits, each encompassing persons of restricted socio-economic status. Indeed, to the individual immigrant the city presents a wide range of opportunities. Immigrants can, as many illiterate and unskilled workers do, maintain social relationships, except for those of the workplace and market, only with members of their town ethnic group or home community. On the other hand, they may consciously exploit to the full the opportunities offered by town life, rejecting relationships with kin and past friends when these seem to be a handicap to further achievement. No matter what strategy immigrants adopt, as long as they maintain links with their rural communities, the rural orientation (which has nothing to do with peasant conservatism) will continue to contribute toward the modification or reinforcement of their aspirations, orientations and expectations.

The three cities represented in this study - Abidjan, Accra and Lagos - are similar in many respects. First, they are capital cities. In addition they are the main commercial centres and premier ports. Consequently a great deal of commercial, industrial, administrative and political activities are concentrated within them, and it is not surprising that they have acted like magnets to the vast majority of disaffected rural dwellers, whose steady arrival has contributed to significant annual increases in the urban population. In Accra, for instance, an average annual population growth rate of 8 per cent between 1950 and 1970 increased the number of residents from 150,000 in 1952 to 636,000 in 1970. A similar picture exists in Abidjan, where the population grew from 126,000 in 1955 to 555,000 in 1970 (an average growth rate of 10 per cent p.a.). In Lagos, where the figure has been about 9 per cent p.a., the population numbered 333,000 in 1952 and 2,500,000 in 1976. These rapid growth rates mean that the cities offer immense advantages for industrial activities, such as local markets for goods, support services and a pool of experienced labour - to which the concentration of manufacturing establishments therein is a testimony. Although in 1980 Nigeria had nine cities with populations over 500,000, 35 per cent of all manufacturing establishments were located in Lagos. At the same time, 30.43 per cent of all Ghana's factories were in Accra (there were two cities with populations over 500,000), while in Côte d'Ivoire, Abidjan - the only city of this size - contained 62.5 per cent of the country's factories.

In addition to providing a concentration of employment opportunities, these cities encompass a wide range of social conditions and living standards. There is a very obvious disparity between the residential areas inhabited by the elites and those that house the urban masses. According to Rao (1974):

> Among those referred to as the urban poor are:
>
> 1 self-employed persons in the service sector (the often-cited hawker, shoe-shine boy, repair and maintenance workers, barbers);
> 2 unskilled workers who are employed in the manufacturing, construction or service sectors - some of them in the modern sector - perhaps irregularly;
> 3 recent migrants who have taken on casual work while looking for better jobs;
> 4 skilled workers, usually self-employed, some of whom have relatively obsolete skills (pottery and hand-spinning) and do not enjoy much demand for their products; others such as tailors and carpenters, who operate on a small scale;
> 5 aged and disabled persons who are not in the labour force - in developing countries they are usually dependents rather than independent households.
>
> Conversely, the urban poor usually exclude skilled operatives in modern industry, government employees, working

> proprietors (even of small firms with few employees), the educated unemployed and those in technical and professional occupations. In general, unionised employees are not among the poor.

There has been a marked trend toward downward mobility since the Rao study, and recent studies of poor urban neighbourhoods in West Africa have consistently shown 'the similarity of lifestyle among households of workers and non-workers'. It is extremely difficult to distinguish workers as an exclusive category in such neighbourhoods. A 1982 ILO study, which categorized 'winners and losers' in the Nigerian economy, classified wage workers along with farmers, informal sector operators and street sellers as 'losers'. The study states 'When we say that a certain group has "lost" we mean that group lost compared to other groups. That is, it did not experience the increase in its real income compared to others.' It is not difficult to generalize this characterization to other West African countries. The majority of rural dwellers as well as the greater proportion of urban dwellers are clearly impoverished, a situation that has worsened in recent years. The industrial workers in this study come from this impoverished social milieu.

Background Characteristics of Respondents

The demographic characteristics of the sample of employees are very important because they disclose relevant aspects of the employees' biographies, which can be related subsequently to their attitudes and feelings, permitting insights into some of the most compelling determinants of action. In other words, the main concern here is to identify and examine important social or background characteristics of the sample. As noted above, 575 questionnaires were analysed for the study; 216 from the Lagos factory, 184 from Accra, and 173 from Abidjan. Of this total number of respondents, the great majority (83.4 per cent) were male, women being uniformly under-represented in all three samples. This is a reflection of the comparatively fewer number of women in semi-skilled factory employment throughout the region. Although there are indications that more women are joining the formal employment sector in West Africa, they are still grossly under-represented in the industrial labour force. In Nigeria, for instance, the 1963 census put the average labour-force participation rate at 88 per cent for men and 27.7 per cent for women, and the same proportions hold true for other countries in the region. The reasons usually advanced for the small number of women in wage employment include their late entry into the labour market, partly as a result of cultural restrictions, religious considerations or early marriage.

More specifically, however, the semi-skilled jobs we are concerned with here are of a strenuous nature, requiring long periods of standing and attending a continually moving machine. Managers are usually reluctant to hire women for these types of jobs. A supervisor in Accra reported that his firm tried employing a few women on the assembly line, but that the experiment failed after the first month. One-third of the women wanted to be moved elsewhere, and by the third month, all had either been moved or had left the company. It would appear that the pace of the assembly line proved too much for this group of women workers. In general, those female respondents included in the sample were working in support jobs (i.e., to the production operatives) and in the packaging divisions.

While sex is an important social characteristic, perhaps age is the most generally relevant background characteristic. Age is very important because it says something about an individual's experiences. It indicates the person's generation and a great deal about the period through which they have lived. The age distribution of workers in the three factories indicates that the production staff are relatively young. In the Lagos factory, about 63 per cent are between the ages of 21 and 30 years, while about 74 per cent of the

Abidjan sample and 53 per cent of the Accra sample are also in this age category. The relative youthfulness of the samples could be explained by two facts; first, economic development is both recent and localized in the largest cities, and modern factories using relatively complex technologies tend to attract younger and better-educated workers; and secondly by the occupational mobility that exists in urban centres. Older workers tend to move up the occupational ladder, move to other jobs or go into self-employment.

The implications of a youthful industrial labour force are of great significance. Most of these workers will have been socialized in an urban milieu and will definitely have a different outlook from the earlier generation of workers who experienced European colonization. The exposure of the younger generation of industrial workers to the rapid changes of urban life is bound to influence their aspirations and expectations. This fact is even more significant because this generation is also fairly well educated (52% of the Lagos sample had secondary education; 19% had been to technical school and 13.4% to polytechnic or university; the figures for Accra were 39.7%, 10.3% and 13.6%; and 42.8%, 15% and 8.1% for Abidjan).

Although most workers in all three sample groups had had some form of education, the Abidjan sample contained the highest number of respondents (11 per cent), who reported having had no formal education at all, in contrast to only 2.8 per cent of the Lagos sample and 6 per cent of the Accra sample. The uneducated Abidjan workers were mainly migrants from rural villages, mostly in the north of the country, and immigrants from neighbouring countries, particularly Mali and Burkina Faso. Furthermore, these were individuals who were originally employed in the factory or in similar organizations as unskilled manual labour but who had nevertheless accumulated enough experience to move up to semi-skilled machine-tending jobs. However, the single largest educated group in each of the three samples was that with a secondary school education. The size of this group in the Lagos sample (52.8 per cent), was partly a reflection of established company policy of hiring only persons with secondary education for this type of job. In both Accra and Abidjan, no such policy existed, although more educated applicants are applying for semi-skilled jobs in increasing numbers. One interesting, and perhaps very significant, feature of the educational distribution is the number of respondents who claimed to have university or polytechnic qualifications. This curious phenomenon is particularly noticeable in the Lagos and Accra samples. It is a well-known fact that more educated people are being produced by the education systems in Nigeria and Ghana than there are jobs being created. In a situation of acute unemployment, educational qualifications are devalued and people are forced to take on any job, at least temporarily, in order to survive. One striking example of this is the fact that the receptionist to the Managing Director's office in the Accra firm had a diploma from a Ghanaian polytechnic. A similar situation appears to be developing in Abidjan, although the massive presence of foreign immigrant workers willing to accept any type of job, irrespective of their qualifications, obscures the extent of the phenomenon among native Ivorians. Ideally, semi-skilled jobs that do not require much technical competence and training are suited to and indeed popular among young secondary school or technical school leavers. Any qualification above this level will prove counter-productive in the long term.

Although relatively young people form the predominant age group in the sample, about 65 per cent of the total sample are married, which implies family responsibilities that affect workers' attitudes and behaviour (the attitude of a single worker towards aspects of life both on and off the job is very likely to differ from that of a married worker with children). A close examination of the distribution according to marital status in the three samples reveals a slight variation in the Abidjan sample, in which a larger proportion of respondents reported that they were single (39.9%, compared with 30.5% and 37.3% in the Lagos and Accra samples, respectively). These figures could reflect the significant numbers of immigrant workers in Abidjan, many of whom come to Côte d'Ivoire alone in search of jobs. When they have saved enough money to marry, they return home. These workers belong to the age group for whom there is heavy family pressure to marry and raise a family - the tendency to marry relatively young is still strong in West Africa.

The individual's marital status is linked to household size, which is important because it gives an idea of the amount of responsibility shouldered by each worker. (In addition to being responsible for members of their immediate household, workers may also be subject to additional demands from individuals and relatives living elsewhere, and for whom they are partly or fully financially responsible, but these dependants are not counted as household members here.) A sizeable proportion of the Lagos sample (23.6 per cent) reported that they lived alone, compared with 5.3 per cent and 5.8 per cent for the Accra and Abidjan respondents, respectively. This is a puzzling finding because the extended family system is still very much in evidence throughout the region. It would appear, however, that in Lagos there is a growing trend for workers to repudiate the stranglehold that the extended family system exerted on the earlier generation of urban workers.

In general, household size is fairly small, consisting of less than eight people. From our observations, these households are increasingly being made up of the worker and his nuclear family and occasionally one or two relatives. Unmarried employees either live alone as is the case in Lagos, or with their parents. In Abidjan, it is more usual for single workers to live with other workers who are friends and share the rent.

Family responsibilities influence behaviour at work in several particularly important ways. On the one hand, workers with families are less likely to engage in disruptive activities in a situation of widespread unemployment. They are also likely to be predisposed to changes in the work environment that could bring in more money to meet their financial obligations. On the other hand, if the rewards from the job prove inadequate to meet these responsibilities, the result could be job dissatisfaction and a lack of commitment. Japanese industry has developed an imaginative solution to this problem, by grading and paying workers according to their age and the extent of their family responsibilities.

Much of the existing literature gives the impression that the majority of workers are migrants from rural areas who are driven from their villages for a variety of reasons, among which economic necessity predominates. Relatively few studies have pointed out that increasing numbers of workers are born and socialized in an urban milieu, as the data from the present study confirms. In the early 1980s, about 65 per cent of the Lagos employees were born either in cities or towns, compared with 71 per cent and 63 per cent of the Accra and Abidjan employees, respectively. This indicates a consolidation of the trend toward urbanization, the previous generation of urban dwellers having established residence in the urban centres while a new generation is emerging whose links with the rural areas are tenuous at best. Nevertheless, this does not imply that migration from the rural villages is slowing down, but rather that new immigrants find it increasingly difficult to secure jobs because of competition from urban-born individuals who have the requisite knowledge of the job market and the 'connections' to seize opportunities as soon as they are available. Traditional norms and values could be expected to exert less of an impact on this new generation, which would more readily conform to Inkeles and Smith's (1960) description of 'modern man'. We must note, however, that a higher proportion of the Lagos employees (31.9 per cent) migrated from rural villages than employees in either the Accra sample (28.8 per cent) or the Abidjan sample (24.8 per cent), and gave the search for jobs as the main reason for their migration.

Some background characteristics impinge on the type of job these individuals are doing. Officially all employees represented in the three samples are classified as *semi-skilled* operatives. When we asked them to classify *themselves,* however, the results were interesting. A substantial number of the Lagos and Abidjan employees (16.2 and 17.9 per cent, respectively) saw themselves as *unskilled* workers in spite of their official categorization as semi-skilled. This downward self-perception of their jobs is perhaps influenced by the fact that outside the factory their acquired skills cannot be applied to any other occupation except one that makes use of similar machinery. According to an employee in Accra:

> Management calling us semi-skilled is not true because you are either skilled, when you have a handwork or unskilled, when you have no handwork. The carpenters who were in our factory have handwork. When they are sacked they can stand on their own. But we have no handwork so if we are sacked we become applicants again.

Logical though the argument is, few of this respondent's co-workers subscribed to it, as the greatest numbers (44.9 per cent for Lagos, 45.7 per cent for Accra, and 48 per cent for Abidjan) considered themselves *skilled* workers. In a non-technological environment, of which West Africa is a good example, machines are generally held in awe and anybody who operates complex machines is usually regarded as skilled. Clearly many of these workers have come to regard themselves in this light - as skilled workers operating complicated machinery. That fact notwithstanding, more of the Accra employees (52.7 per cent) correctly saw themselves as semi-skilled, while similarly, only a tiny proportion (1.6 per cent) of the same sample considered themselves as being unskilled.

A related factor is the length of time that these employees have spent in their present jobs. The majority of employees in the samples (66.5 per cent in Lagos, 54.4 per cent in

Accra, 72.8 per cent in Abidjan) had spent less than five years in their job, a distribution more pronounced in the Abidjan firm. As noted earlier, the sample is predominantly of a young age group, and these workers had not accrued much seniority of service. The length of service distribution further reflects the average age of the Abidjan firm, where about 96 per cent of semi-skilled workers had been in their jobs for less than ten years. The other two groups of respondents also reflect this distribution, but to a lesser degree (87 per cent in Accra, 86 per cent in Lagos). The implication is that there is still a degree of upward and sideways mobility, although company records in the three firms indicate that the workforces are fairly stable.

Respondents were almost equally divided about whether they underwent any training or not. This is understandable because there is no formal training at all in each of the three firms, at least initially. A new employee is simply attached to another worker and after a few days is deemed to have learned enough to go on the assembly line. For some respondents - 47.7 per cent for the Lagos firm, 45.1 per cent for Accra and 45.7 per cent for the Abidjan firm - this counts as training - after all, a certain amount of knowledge about the job is transmitted, albeit in an informal and unstructured fashion. When respondents were asked if they had learnt any new skill on the job, the majority said they had (69.9 per cent in Lagos, 76.1 per cent in Accra, 61.3 per cent in Abidjan). However, more of the Accra respondents (54.9 per cent) reported that they had received no training than those who said they had. The Lagos respondents were almost evenly divided. A sizeable proportion of the Abidjan employees (15.6 per cent) did not respond to the question, and 18.5 per cent did not know whether they had acquired a new skill or not (10.3 per cent in Accra, 7 per cent in Lagos).

Finally, to complete the picture, we look at parental background, and specifically at the father's education and occupation. The employee's parental background can tell us many things. It indicates the type of schooling a worker would have had, indicates life-chances, and perhaps determines future opportunities for social mobility. In the very recent past West African countries were relatively open societies where 'rags to riches' experiences were often the rule rather than the exception. A study by Imoagene (1974) found that in the late 1960s most of the elite groups in Nigeria had parents who were engaged in rural occupations with little or no formal education. However, that open society is gradually but steadily closing up. Upward mobility is becoming more difficult, especially for individuals who lack the necessary family support. In the three firms, slightly less than half of the employees had fathers who had no formal education, followed in each case by those whose fathers had primary education. The implication here is that those individuals born in urban centres were likely to have had fathers employed in manual or low-level white-collar jobs. Those born in the rural areas would most likely be children of farmers (39.4 per cent of the Lagos sample, 45.1 per cent of the Accra sample, and 34.1 per cent of the Abidjan sample). In fact, the largest category of respondents reported that their fathers were farmers. Similarly, a sizeable proportion reported that their fathers were or had been traders (20.4 per cent in Lagos, 14.7 per cent in Accra, 19.7 per cent in Abidjan). More of the Accra and Abidjan respondents had fathers who were better educated than the Lagos sample, and this is reflected in the father's occupation: 22.3 per cent of the Accra sample and 18.5 per cent of the Abdijan sample had fathers who were teachers or civil servants, compared with 14.4 per cent of the Lagos sample. The group classified as 'others' included those whose fathers were dead, unemployed or engaged in the professions, for example law, and accounted for 16.2 per cent of the Lagos sample, 13 per cent in Accra, 22.8 per cent in Abidjan.

It is obvious that respondents from the three different firms and cities had many background characteristics in common and we can make certain relatively valid generalizations on this basis. Our sample consists of semi-skilled factory operatives tending assembly-line machines. They are largely male, young, fairly well educated and, more often than not, born in an urban area. They are second- (possibly third-) generation urban workers whose fathers usually had little or no education, and many consider themselves to be skilled workers. As noted earlier, the individual's performance is a consequence of two factors - the ability and the motivation to work. We maintained that ability stemmed from knowledge and skill, which were influenced by education, experience, training and interest. From the social characteristics presented above, it is reasonable to conclude that the sample rated fairly high in terms of ability. But these young, educated employees were engaged in jobs where the degree of aptitude and level of training required are fairly low. Thus the major variable that will determine their performance on the job is *motivation*. The next chapter deals with the factors that affect the individual's motivation at work.

6 Factors Affecting Worker Behaviour

Social Factors

Two sets of factors must be taken into consideration if worker behaviour is to be properly understood. These are social factors and job factors, and the interaction of the two determines motivation at work. Where these factors are congruent, the employee is highly motivated, and vice versa. The social factors that are considered here refer primarily to those *outside* the work environment, but whose effects are crucial to work performance. These factors arise from and are grounded in the worker's life outside the factory gates.

Salient Needs

It has become fairly commonplace in the study of organizational behaviour to look at the needs of employees in terms of a hierarchy. This is an important legacy of Abraham Maslow's theory (see figure 6.1), which postulated that all human needs can be arranged in an ascending hierarchy, and that the lowest levels of needs that are left unsatisfied are the main motivators of individuals. The lowest-level needs are physiological - essential needs that include food, water, clothing, housing, and so on. These must be met to some extent before an individual can even begin to think of other needs. If they are satisfied, the needs of the next level in the hierarchy become the motivating factors. As long as low-level needs remain unsatisfied, an individual is dominated by them and cannot be concerned with needs of a higher order.

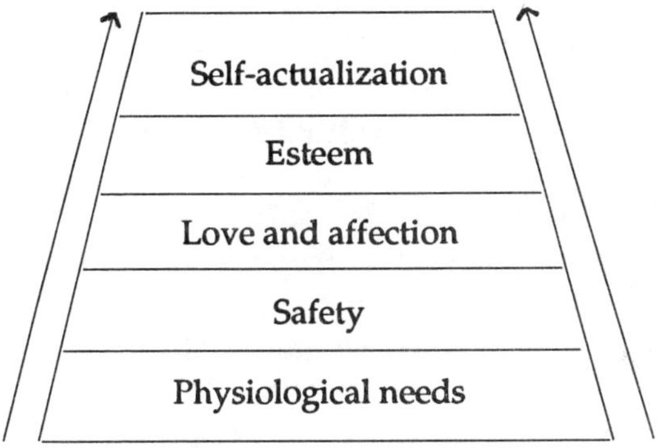

Figure 6.1 Maslow's hierarchy of needs

The next level above physiological needs consists of safety needs, which include job security and various forms of insurance against the risk of occupational fatality, accident and injury. If these needs are satisfied, the worker becomes concerned with needs of the next level - for love and affection. To satisfy these needs, the individual seeks close relationships with family and friends. If these needs are met, needs of esteem then demand attention: most people have a desire for esteem from others as well as self-respect for themselves. The highest need identified in the hierarchy is the desire for self-actualization - the need of the individual to fulfil potential. However, as a creative urge, this applies only to those *with the capacity* for creation - and Maslow's theory asserts that each level of needs in the hierarchy must be satisfied in part, before higher-level needs become motivating. An individual's behaviour may be determined at any given time by several needs at different levels.

The physiological needs of workers are met primarily through wages. While workers in developed countries usually fulfil these needs, the same cannot be said for workers in developing countries, especially in West Africa. This has obvious implications for the next level of needs - safety needs - as motivators of action. Safety needs depend largely on job security, and prospects for the individual's future well-being. As these two sets of needs are still very salient in the West African situation, we will focus on them.

In West African urban centres, the most problematic need after food security is shelter. Migrants from rural villages need somewhere to sleep and keep their belongings, while those already in the towns must continually seek better and more spacious accommodation to cater for growing families. A cursory view of most West African cities will show that only a minority of the population - usually the elites - have adequate housing facilities. The rest have to make do with whatever is available. Government attempts to build low-cost housing in the past have not been very successful, and a minority of companies try to provide accommodation for their employees, but this is very limited. The three firms represented in the sample do not provide accommodation for low-level employees.

Using a concept of housing that includes the area where the employee lives, distance from the workplace, the rent paid and the quality of nearby schools, in addition to the size and physical condition of the dwelling itself, employees were asked how satisfied they were with these aspects of their present accommodation. House size is very important, depending on the number of people staying there. It is quite common for a family of six or more to live in a one-room apartment in West African cities. In such a situation, there is scarcely room for an individual to move about, and sleeping arrangements are often cramped and awkward. It is doubtful whether a worker living in such a confined apartment would regard it as good accommodation, but in the absence of an alternative would have to be satisfied with it all the same: 15.5 per cent and 12.7 per cent of the Lagos and Abidjan samples, respectively, reported that they were *very dissatisfied* with the size of their houses, compared with only 3.3 per cent of the Accra sample. As low-income housing is very scarce in Lagos and Abidjan, workers do not generally leave it unless they die, are transferred out of town, or retire to the villages. Housing construction, which has slowed down during the current economic decline, does not keep pace with demand. An even bigger proportion of the three samples say they were *dissatisfied* with the size of their houses. More Accra employees (41.8 per cent) than employees in the other two groups fall into this category, compared with 26.9 per cent and 22.5 per cent for Lagos and Abidjan, respectively. In Accra, visits to low-income areas revealed crowded houses with numerous people milling around at all times of the day. The situation here is far worse than conditions observed in Lagos and Abidjan. Although working-class districts were crowded in Abidjan as well, there was evidence that some effort was being made to keep the environment neat and tidy, an approach definitely missing in Accra and to some extent in Lagos. A large number of respondents from Accra were indifferent to the size of their houses, that is they expressed no opinion on the matter. Similarly, a sizeable proportion of the Abidjan employees (24.3 per cent) could not decide whether they were satisfied or not, compared with only 11.6 per cent for the Lagos sample. However, more Lagos employees were either satisfied or very satisfied with the size of their houses (46 per cent) closely followed by the Abidjan sample (40.4 per cent) and only 18.5 per cent for Accra. The opinions expressed by these workers are closely related to the rate at which urban housing facilities become available in relation to demand. Ghana has had a longer experience of economic problems, which have had a serious impact on the construction industry: fewer houses for low-income groups are being built in the urban centres, while unabated migration to the towns stretches available facilities to the limit. The same situation exists in Lagos and Abidjan as well, but to a lesser extent.

The physical condition of the dwelling is related to its size. A visit to many low-income urban areas will reveal rickety and unmaintained houses packed with people. About one third of respondents in all three samples felt they were dissatisfied or very dissatisfied with the condition of their homes. Again it is significant that 39.1 per cent of the Accra sample expressed no opinion, followed by 34.7 per cent of the Abidjan employees. Abidjan was the best-maintained of the three cities. Even the low-income areas showed evidence of attempts to keep them neat, yet the single largest category of employees in the Abidjan sample had no opinion about whether they liked or disliked the condition of their houses. Lagos had the largest proportion of respondents (38.4 per cent) who reported that they were satisfied with the physical condition of their homes. One possible explanation for the large number of people who expressed no opinion on this issue could be that living in the same apartment for a long period of time induces feelings of apathy towards poor conditions. In addition, physical conditions do not become an issue for many of the respondents, who share their homes with numerous others, as long as the dwellings fulfil the function of providing shelter. Most houses in a given area look alike, and because deterioration over time is at an even pace it often passes unnoticed.

Such housing is found in specific areas throughout all three cities, which harbour a range of conditions, living standards and styles. There is a hierarchical ordering of urban space in these cities that largely coincides with the division of labour determined by the dominant capitalist mode of production. There are residential areas for the elites in government, the military and in business - Victoria Island or Ikoyi in Lagos, the GRA in Accra or the Plateau in Abidjan. There are usually several residential quarters that cater for low-income workers, artisans, traders, the unemployed, and so on. Treichville in Abidjan and Ajegunle in Lagos are good examples. There are better social facilities - roads, water, electricity - in the well-laid-out elite residential areas than in the crowded low-income quarters. Nevertheless, very few respondents in each of the three samples reported that they felt very dissatisfied with the area in which they lived (7 per cent in Lagos, 5.4 per cent in Accra, 3.5 per cent in Abidjan), while another relatively small proportion reported being dissatisfied: again the Accra sample was the largest in this respect with 23.4 per cent, while 17.6 per cent were dissatisfied in Lagos and 11.3 per cent in Abidjan. On average, 42.6 per cent of respondents in all three firms felt quite satisfied with the neighbourhoods in which they lived. This might appear anomalous: how can people be satisfied with areas that are definitely disadvantaged in comparison with the elite areas? The explanation is quite simple. The low-income areas are vibrant and full of life. An employee in Abidjan who lives in the popular Treichville said:

> I will not even think of going to live in the place where the big men live. In that place you can stay one whole day and see nobody. It is not the way of the African. We were brought up in a compound full of people. We were always surrounded by people and here in Treichville, though our conditions are not too good, this is where the life is.

These residential quarters are alive until very late at night. Throughout the day, record shops play music, the bars are open, doing good business, and street traders and hawkers are everywhere. It is easy to be carried away by the sheer exuberance of living in these urban ghettoes, in spite of the dirt, the lack of most basic amenities and the overcrowding.

Most of these low-income urban areas in West Africa develop around areas of employment, near the docks, the railway yards, the mines or industrial estates. They do have one major advantage - they are near to the workplace. This is substantiated by the proportion of respondents who are satisfied with the distance between their place of residence and their place of work. Some 43.5 per cent of the Lagos respondents, 50.5 per cent of Accra respondents and 45.7 per cent of the Abidjan sample said they were satisfied with this aspect of their housing situation. The crucial advantage of proximity to the workplace is that it significantly reduces the cost of getting to work. It must be said, however, that a sizeable proportion of respondents reported being dissatisfied with the distance to their places of work, especially in Lagos, where 28.7 per cent were dissatisfied and 8.3 per cent very dissatisfied. Travelling any distance is a big problem in Lagos, where traffic is usually quite chaotic at all times of the day, and the newer low-income residential quarters are located at greater distances from centres of employment. However, this may be compensated for to some extent by what is now normal practice for many companies - the provision of staff buses. The Lagos firm in our sample provides huge buses for its staff, but the frequent complaint is that they arrive very early in the morning in order to avoid the heaviest morning traffic, and employees have the inconvenience of waking up very early to prepare for work. This situation is also true for Accra and Abidjan, but to a much lesser degree.

Rent is another factor that has far-reaching implications for housing. Any savings that an employee might glean from the proximity of home to the workplace may be lost in the form of rent. Rent consumes a major part of the monthly expenditure, except for those employees who are lucky enough to be provided with company housing (none in the three samples) or those who live in government-built low-income housing. As our samples confirm, rent is more of a problem for employees in Lagos than in Abidjan, where government rent controls are more effective. Some 19 per cent of Lagos respondents are very dissatisfied with the amount of rent they pay, compared with only 2.7 per cent and 1.2 per cent in Accra and Abidjan, respectively. Government rent controls have been attempted unsuccessfully in Lagos on a number of occasions. Most low-income housing is owned by individuals who charge whatever they consider adequate as rent, and since there are more tenants than houses, people have no choice but to pay up. Thus 49.1 per cent were dissatisfied in the Lagos sample, 35.3 per cent in Accra and 24.9 per cent in Abidjan, but an even larger proportion expressed no opinion (37.5 per cent in Accra, 37 per cent in Abidjan). It should come as no surprise that more Abidjan respondents (31.2 per cent) reported satisfaction with the amount of rent they paid.

The quality of nearby schools is also associated with the type of area in which respondents live. As already noted, low-income areas come out worse in the distribution of social facilities and infrastructure. Government-provided resources are often inadequate and cannot cope with the increasing demands put upon them by a growing urban population. Schools are very important to West African workers, and there is general recognition of the importance of education as a route to upward social mobility, as evidenced by the huge increases in educational enrolment that have taken place since independence in all West African countries. We sought the opinion of respondents as to the quality of schools in their areas, finding that only a very small minority were very dissatisfied (6 per cent in Lagos, 0.5 per cent in Accra, 6.4 per cent in Abidjan), while another small proportion stated that they were dissatisfied (17.6 per cent, 4.3 per cent, and 12.7 per cent, respectively). However, a comparatively large proportion expressed no opinion (24.6 per cent in Lagos, 51.2 per cent in Accra and 32.9 per cent in Abidjan) - a response that could indicate either that a large number of respondents were uninformed about the quality of nearby schools, perhaps because they had had no contact with them, or that they were indifferent to the issue of schooling. In the case of the large Accra category, it would appear that the problem was one of indifference. Many respondents shrugged when asked this question and some replied that it was of no consequence. It is likely that those respondents in each of the samples who had no opinion on the quality of schools in their areas probably had no children of school age, and were unable to make an evaluation. However, for those individuals who had children in school, a larger proportion stated that they were satisfied with school provision in their area (36.1 per cent in Lagos, 32.6 per cent in Accra, 22.5 per cent in Abidjan).

Even though a larger proportion of the sample tended to be satisfied with various aspects of housing, a significant number expressed degrees of dissatisfaction. Employees tend to be satisfied with jobs that fulfil important needs, one of the most important being housing. Nevertheless, life in urban centres creates other needs that come to be regarded as basic as well. For instance, an individual living in the city requires a means of acquiring information, a radio set, and a watch or clock to keep track of time. These are not as important to a rural inhabitant as they are to the city dweller, who sees them as necessities. They also bestow prestige on their owners, who would be considered failures if they lacked such trappings of modernism. We asked workers in the three cities to indicate which of the following domestic appliances and consumer items they possessed: radio, tape recorder or record player, television set, refridgerator, watch or clock, electric fan. On average, over 80 per cent possessed a radio, clock or watch, 71 per cent an electric fan, 49 per cent a tape recorder or record player, 45 per cent a television set (in Lagos 76 per cent had television), and 29 per cent a refridgerator.

These appliances are not only important items of convenience and prestige to urban employees, but are also used by economists as indices of modernity: the number of radios in a given population denotes it as modernized or backward. A radio is the most common item and has great value. It is the first item an urban worker seeks to buy once employment is secured. It is the cheapest means of keeping abreast of information and music. Not surprisingly, most respondents reported having a radio, but fewer had a tape recorder or record player in their houses (41.4 per cent for the Lagos sample, 43.4 per cent for the Abidjan sample, 56.5 per cent in

Accra). Audio equipment is relatively expensive and calls for substantial savings. Although many employees considered that owning a radio was enough for them, they would not have minded owning tape recorders or record players if the possibility had arisen.

A television set is the most sought-after item, but is beyond the reach of many workers. More of the Lagos respondents (76.9 per cent) reported owning television sets compared with 41.3 per cent in Accra and 49.1 per cent in Abidjan. Until very recently, television sets were very cheap in Lagos, especially those made in Taiwan and Korea, and most individuals interested in buying one could get a small black-and-white set for as little as 80 dollars. There was, and still is, a thriving market in electronic goods, especially television sets from Lagos offered for sale in Accra and Abidjan where they fetch very high prices. Most respondents in Accra and Abidjan report not having television sets (58.7 per cent, and 50.9 per cent, respectively). This also applies to refridgerators, which require a huge capital outlay and are usually a long-term project for most low-income earners. Some 31 per cent of the Lagos sample, along with 28.8 per cent of the Accra and 30.5 per cent of the Abidjan samples stated that they owned a refridgerator, while the vast majority did not. The cheapest item, and one of the most important to workers is a watch or clock, which helps immeasurably with time-keeping, prompt reporting for work, signing off, and so on. Without a time-piece, the employee is seriously handicapped in an environment where time and punctuality are important values to be observed. As our average figures showed, almost all respondents in the Lagos and Abidjan samples had a watch or clock. However, more of the Accra respondents reported not owning one (27.2 per cent, compared with 9.7 per cent in Lagos and 8.1 per cent in Abidjan). The electric fan is another most useful and important item to have in the hot and humid climate of West Africa, an environment compounded by the crowded nature of urban low-income housing. It does not require much capital outlay compared with a refridgerator or television set. Some 80.6 per cent of the Lagos sample reported having an electric fan. Of the Accra and Abidjan respondents, the majority reported having fans but a sizeable proportion had none (37 per cent and 38.7 per cent, respectively). Generally, these modern domestic appliances make the worker's after-work hours more comfortable and help promote relaxation and recuperation from the stresses of work. They also confer social prestige and feelings of accomplishment on their owners. Their absence will heighten dissatisfaction, especially if workers' peers have somehow managed to obtain a number of these items.

The discussion so far suggests that, in terms of workers' basic needs as measured by housing and the possession of a number of essential modern items, things were inadequate and could be improved considerably. Many employees in all three firms were in an uncomfortable situation as far as domestic housing was concerned, and still lacked important items that would improve their quality of life and make them amenable to management and government calls for increased productivity. Employees tend to look at the employment relationship as an exchange relationship in which they expect an equitable return for their efforts. When there appears to be an imbalance in the relationship, where the output appears to be always in one direction with no recompense for effort, it is difficult to get them to work harder and more efficiently.

Leisure

In the middle of the nineteenth century, Karl Marx believed that work provided the most important and vital means for an individual to fulfil basic needs, individuality and humanity. Through self-expression in the creation of a product, the worker can experience deep satisfaction. Several studies in the present century, however, have shown that workers are deriving less satisfaction from their work. C. Wright Mills

(1953) noted that 'For most employees work has a generally unpleasant quality. . . .Such joy as creative work may carry is more and more limited to a small minority.' Peter Berger (1964) goes further to suggest a three-fold division of modern work in terms of its human significance. First, there is work that still provides an occasion for primary self-identification and self-commitment of the individual - or 'self-fulfilment' if one prefers. Secondly, there is work that is apprehended as a direct threat to self-identification, an indignity, an oppression. Thirdly, there is work that is neither fulfilment nor oppression, a sort of grey neutral region in which one neither rejoices nor suffers. People endure such work with more or less grace for the sake of other things in their private lives, including leisure. As more people derive less satisfaction from dull routine jobs, they tend to turn to activities outside work. However, leisure is a very difficult concept to define, a task that Young and Wilmott (1973) likened to trying to grasp a jellyfish. For our purposes here, we want to approach the concept from the construct that Stanley Parker (1982) labelled the 'life space'. According to Parker, the 'life space' means the total sum of activities or ways of spending time that people have. He proposed a 'time scheme' as a means of analysing the 'life space' as illustrated in figure 6.2.

Work time		**Non-work time**		
Employment	Work obligations	Physiological needs	Non-work obligations	Leisure

Figure 6.2 Time scheme for analysing life space (in Parker, 1982, p. 10).

The life space has two main components; 'work time' and 'non-work time' or what may be referred to as 'free time' - the period of time that the worker is free from the obligations attendant on the regular job, i.e., the period of time between official closing time and the resumption of work next day. This includes work-free weekends, public holidays and annual vacations. During free time, the worker undertakes certain non-work activities that Dumazedier classified into four categories according to economic needs, social obligations, family duties and recreative and cultural duties. Only if the worker is free from any obligations is it possible to pursue true rewarding leisure. Leisure has important functions for the worker; it provides relaxation and entertainment, and contributes toward releasing the strains of work. True leisure can help make the individual a better adjusted person and, by extension, a better worker. To assess the extent of leisure available to our sample, several factors were taken into consideration. First of all, respondents were asked if they had a hobby.

A surprisingly low proportion of the Lagos and Accra respondents said they had a hobby (20.4 per cent and 27.7 per cent, respectively). The reason commonly given was that hobbies take time and money, both of which were in short supply. However, the Abidjan employees were almost evenly divided between those who had (43.9 per cent) and those who did not (56.1 per cent). A follow-up question as to what these hobbies were elicited a long list of sporting and social activities, most of which we shall discuss later. This general lack of hobbies among these industrial workers differentiates them from British or North American workers who, as the literature suggests, almost always have a hobby of some kind, such as sailing, model-making, photography, and so on. Perhaps the most important reason for this difference is the fact that industrial workers in Britain and North America are much more affluent than their West African counterparts and can afford to devote part of their income to non-money-making hobbies. Workers in our samples were asked to respond to some sporting and social activities that they enjoyed either as participants or as spectators.

Football is by far the most popular sport in most West African countries and draws interest from all segments of society. Nigeria, Ghana and Côte d'Ivoire are all footballing nations so we would expect a high rate of interest among the sample of employees, and indeed, the majority said that they participated in the sport either as players or spectators. Only a comparatively small segment of the total sample (13.9 per cent in Lagos, 26.1 per cent in Accra and 19.1 per cent in Abidjan) stated that they were not interested in football. In many low-income areas, every small space available is converted rapidly to football fields where people congregate to watch or play at evenings and weekends. Television has also become an important medium for keeping up with football matches. Table tennis is another sporting activity that does not require much money, and is most popular among the Lagos respondents, about 72 per cent of whom reported either playing table tennis or watching others play. Most streets in low-income areas have table-tennis boards. For very little cost, an individual can participate in an exciting, energetic, competitive and skilful sport that provides the opportunity to win, increase proficiency and acquire a measure of social acclaim. One board can be used by many people and makes some extra money for the owner in the process. Table tennis is, however, not as popular in Accra and Abidjan as it is in Lagos. About 59.8 per cent of the Accra sample and 43.5 per cent of the Abidjan sample reported having no interest in table tennis and only a very small minority of these two samples said they played.

Abidjan, Accra and Lagos are all coastal cities and one would expect swimming to be a prominent sporting activity. However, as the sample here illustrates, most people were not interested in swimming, (62.5 per cent for Lagos, 56.5 per cent for Accra and 59.5 per cent for Abidjan). It is likely that many of these respondents, who were migrants from the hinterland, could not swim. Swimming lessons are not generally available, and are usually restricted to elite clubs. Whilst a sizeable proportion of the total sample (30.3 per cent) suggested that they watched swimming as sport, only a very small fraction reported that they themselves swam at all. Jogging is perhaps the cheapest of sporting activities, requiring no money and no particular field or area in which to run. It is presented in the mass media as a way of keeping fit and, for a time, was popularized by the late Burkinabe President, Captain Thomas Sankara. In Nigeria, the Federal Government supported jogging as the cheapest way of keeping healthy, but it would appear that these efforts were not very productive, as a majority of the sample did not like jogging (78 per cent for Lagos, 58.8 per cent for Accra, and 60.1 per cent for Abidjan respondents). Again only a very small minority reported taking part in jogging. The reason for this relatively widespread dislike could be that jogging is regarded by this group as an upper-class and slightly ridiculous activity. Many respondents thought it ludicrous for an adult to be seen running about all over the place.

Lawn tennis is even less popular. It requires considerable capital outlay to buy the equipment necessary, a sacrifice that only very few working-class individuals can make: 77.8 per cent of the Lagos sample, 61.2 per cent of the Accra and 77.4 per cent of the Abidjan samples were not interested in lawn tennis. However, a considerable number reported that they watched lawn tennis matches, probably on television, since most low-income areas lack the facilities for participation in such a sport.

Finally, respondents were asked to name other sports in which they were interested. The most important were wrestling, boxing and to a lesser extent basketball. It would appear that sporting interests, with the possible exception of football, did not feature prominently among the leisure activities of our samples in all three cities. The reasons for this are two-fold. First, scarce resources: employees complained that they had many other pressing obligations (physiological, familial, social and cultural) on which to spend their money before they even thought of sporting equipment and activities. Secondly, there are very few facilities available, even for those activities that do not require significant financial outlay. City planners in these low-income residential areas make little provision for public space in which individuals can pursue leisure activities, a factor that denies the greater majority of citizens certain urban privileges.

Leisure is, however, not confined to sporting activities. In fact, one of the most important characteristics of leisure is that it can be either passive or active, solitary or spent in groups. A woman or man who sits quietly in a corner reading an interesting book is pursuing leisure just as much as a group of workers who attend a football match after work. Respondents were asked to indicate from a list of social activities which ones they enjoyed most. Africans are noted for their interest in music - playing it, listening to it and dancing to it - a cultural trait that persists to the present day among people of African descent worldwide. The majority of the total sample reported that they enjoyed listening to music (most reported owning radio sets). Only a very small proportion (10.5 per cent on average), but more in the Abidjan sample (23.7 per cent), said they did not like listening to music.

Just as music is part of the African cultural heritage, so is tilling the soil. Statistics show that in present-day West Africa, farming is still the source of subsistence for most people, so that even urban residents, the majority of whom remain in contact with their rural homes, still retain the farming tradition. As gardening in this sense is labour rather than a leisure activity, most respondents reported that they did not enjoy gardening (56.5 per cent in Lagos, 57.6 per cent in Accra and 59.5 per cent in Abidjan). Lack of space could be a major hindrance here too. In low-income urban areas, every available space is usually taken up with buildings, leaving very little for those who are interested in gardening, as 43.5, 42.4 and 39.9 per cent of the Lagos, Accra and Abidjan respondents indicated that they were.

If gardening is not very popular, drinking is, and it has also been identified in Africa as one of the major problems with the African worker. Two examples of studies that have linked alcoholism to low productivity in Africa have already been discussed elsewhere. This problem is not confined to Africa alone, however, and recent disclosures in the Soviet press indicate a deep-seated and widespread problem of alcoholism among Soviet workers. Our interest is not in alcoholism but in drinking as a social activity: millions of people throughout the world drink alcohol, but only a small minority become alcoholics. Responses to our questionnaires indicate that drinking was more popular with the Abidjan respondents (61.8 per cent) than among the Lagos and Accra respondents (36.1 per cent and 39.7 per cent, respectively). This finding supports the study quoted by Sandbrook (1982), which identified drinking as one of the major reasons for low productivity, absenteeism and high staff turnover among 1,000 manual workers in Abidjan. Alcohol can be used as an avenue of escape from the daily struggle to survive in a hostile, unkind urban environment. As La Fontaine (1970) noted, town life is highly competitive and the results of failure are readily apparent. The living conditions of the urban dweller are subject to changes brought about by economic and political forces that may not be comprehended, but which nevertheless have profound effects. In the struggle to succeed, the individual is both more isolated and more independent than in a traditional setting, and it would be easy for some individuals to resort to drinking. However, this does not explain why fondness for drinking was higher among the Abidjan respondents, nor does the common argument that French-speaking Africans drink more than other Africans, although a great deal of literature seems to point in this direction. Perhaps a more plausible explanation would be that social tolerance of drinking is higher in Abidjan and among French-speaking countries generally. Whatever the explanation, it is a problem that requires further study. Among the Lagos sample, 63.9 per cent reported they did not enjoy drinking, compared with 60.3 per cent in Accra, and 38.2 per cent in Abidjan.

Watching television is a passive leisure activity that has tremendous potential. All that is required is the original investment to purchase a set. Furthermore, it is not necessary to go outside the home to watch television and the pastime has significance for family and social relationships. Theoretically, interesting and exciting programmes have the potential to bring family members and sometimes close neighbours together, further strengthening existing social ties. Most respondents in the three firms report that they enjoy watching television, and perhaps the availability of sets might be a constraint among the proportion that report they do not enjoy watching it. With imaginative programming, television has the potential to serve as a major leisure source for all segments of any society.

Most developed societies have a 'reading culture', which implies that many citizens have a habit of reading books that interest them. Periodic polls conducted in the United States monitor increases and declines in the rate of reading per person. The same kind of reading culture does not exist in West African countries. For most people outside the educational institutions, reading is restricted to official documents, newspapers, and for a minority the occasional book. The distribution of respondents who were asked whether they enjoyed reading or not shows that more people in the Lagos and Accra samples (73.6 per cent and 70.1 per cent, respectively), enjoyed reading, compared with 30.6 per cent of the Abidjan sample. For some reason, a reading culture has yet to prove itself attractive to this sector of the population. It is possible that they spend more time on other activities such as drinking and have little time left for such 'unprofitable' pursuits as reading. Visiting friends could be a source of both entertainment and distraction, although it could also prove to be expensive in terms of transportation costs. More people in the Lagos and Abidjan samples (57.4 per cent and 46.8 per cent, respectively) said they enjoyed visiting friends, while most people in the Accra sample (61.4 per cent) said they did not. Furthering one's education through night school has been a well-tested avenue to upward social mobility, yet most of the sample (81 per cent in Accra, 76.3 per cent in Abidjan, and slightly less in the Lagos sample - 64.8 per cent) reported that they did not attend evening classes. Similarly, very few people (11.6 per cent in the Lagos sample, 7.6 per cent in Accra, and more in the Abidjan sample - 22.5 per cent) suggested that they would rather stay idle during their free time, while a larger proportion - over 50 per cent in Accra and Abidjan, and 75.5 per cent in the Lagos sample - reported that they attended religious places regularly.

As we have noted, leisure activities for these employees are circumscribed by two factors - lack of resources and lack of facilities. Employees were asked to identify those facilities available to them in their areas of residence, and their responses confirmed this paucity of provision. Of all the facilities listed (playing fields, cinema, theatre, drinking bars, swimming pools, community centres) only bars were reported to be generally available by the three groups of respondents. Playing fields were available to about half the respondents in Lagos and Accra and about two-thirds of the Abidjan sample. Cinemas were available to 71.7 per cent in Abidjan and by only 30.4 per cent of respondents in Accra, while very few had access to theatres (6.4 per cent) in Abidjan and some 16 per cent in the other two cities. The same is true for swimming pools and community centres where people can meet and play indoor games. The paucity of urban recreational amenities in low-income residential areas puts serious limits on residents' options of leisure pursuits, with obvious implications for the close relationship that has been postulated between work performance and leisure. We expect employees who have adequate and meaningful leisure to be better adjusted citizens who are willing to work as hard as possible at monotonous jobs, as long as these provide the means to pursue more interesting activities outside work. Where this is not the case, workers carry the frustrations of the working day home with them, find no outlet in leisure pursuits during non-working hours, and then carry them right back to work again. One major consequence could be a tense mood in the workplace, and quarrelsome employees who are ready to take offence at any slight provocation and end up being mediocre producers. It is only when the workers' 'many needs, for interest, for meaning, for a sense of participation and of achievement, left unsatisfied by the rationalized jobs performed in the factory, office, mine and workshop' are satisfied in their after-work activities that the full potential of the labour force can begin to be achieved.

Attitudes to Life

Individuals hold widely divergent attitudes to life in general, depending on their unique experiences of socialization, relationships and personality. Nevertheless, individuals in the same objective situation tend to develop similar attitudes to life - and here we are concerned with membership of a common economic category. If people who are classified as belonging to a particular economic category believe themselves to be exploited and deprived, they are likely to share a negative attitude to life. This said, however, in any group of people there will always be a number who are generally dissatisfied with life, regardless of their circumstances.

Attitudes have a significant bearing on job satisfaction and performance. Bass and Barrett (1973) noted that it is a popular conception that people who are unhappy with life in general compensate by seeking more satisfaction from their job. They 'bury themselves in their work'. The correlational data, however, do not support this 'compensatory' view of job and life satisfaction. Indeed the evidence supports a 'spill-over' of job to life satisfaction or vice versa. In other words, people who are satisfied with their life situation are likely to be satisfied with their job also, while those who achieve job satisfaction are also likely to feel satisfied with life in general. Nevertheless, satisfaction with life depends on the existence of favourable conditions in the individual's environment. As discussed earlier, the social environment of these low-level employees is fraught with hardship and deprivation, a situation in which income, although regular, buys less and less. It is also a condition of insecurity, in which jobs could be lost at very short notice and unemployment become a real problem. Given this environment, what attitudes do workers hold to life? To answer this question, respondents were asked to compare themselves with other citizens in their respective countries and assess how life had treated them.

The majority thought that life had treated them fairly. More of the Lagos respondents (about 83.4 per cent) fell into this category than in Accra (51.6 per cent) and Abidjan (61.8 per cent). In Lagos any employees, and low-level employees in particular, who escaped the retrenchments of 1984-86 would consider themselves lucky to be in regular employment. Statistics from the Nigerian Labour Congress show that since Nigeria's economic problems began, one in four industrial employees has been made redundant. Although the situation has improved somewhat, jobs are still insecure, and to have a job and regular salary is indeed a sign of good fortune in Lagos. The same can be said of the situation in Accra and Abidjan, where widespread unemployment makes getting and keeping a job a major achievement. However, more respondents in these two samples considered that life had not been fair to them - 48.3 per cent of the Accra sample and 38.2 per cent of the Abidjan sample, compared with 16.7 per cent of the Lagos sample. This relatively large number of discontented people could be victims of both absolute and relative impoverishment. Absolute impoverishment is the deterioration of the whole aggregate of workers' working and living conditions as a result of economic forces they cannot understand and feel powerless to influence. Nevertheless, even in the face of a fall in living standards, some segments of the population are living well and actually progressing: relative impoverishment is a worsening of their circumstances compared with other groups in society. It is difficult to justify a situation in which companies declare huge profits at the end of each year while workers consistently receive poorer rewards for their efforts. This is a widespread complaint encountered throughout the three cities visited. There is general disenchantment with the system that permits the bosses, i.e., management, to live well and drive good cars while the workers have nothing. Respondents were asked further whether they believed that a poor man who worked hard would succeed and whether they felt that opportunities for improvement still existed for such a person.

It is very important to determine the degree of faith that these groups of people have in the social and economic systems under which they labour. Western employees are said to operate within the Protestant work ethic, which preaches hard work and the delay of gratification. The system, in turn, guarantees the hard worker adequate returns. Where people have little faith that they will obtain rewards commensurate with their effort, it is difficult to convince them that it is worth putting in any extra energy beyond the necessary minimum. Most respondents believed that a poor man who worked hard enough would probably succeed. While only a small minority in Accra (13.6 per cent) and in Abidjan (5.8 per cent) believed that he would definitely succeed, a sizeable proportion of the Lagos sample, however (37.5 per cent) believed that this outcome was the most likely. To a greater extent than in Accra and Abidjan, the low-income areas of Lagos abound with examples of former employees who became 'business men' and subsequently rich. In fact, the business class was regarded as a model by the majority of Lagos respondents, who dreamt of the day when they could quit wage employment and join the growing group of self-employed business men. It is significant that about 50 per cent of the three samples still believed that a hardworking person would probably succeed in life, perhaps with the additional assistance of luck, prayers and connections. It is also significant that more people in Accra and Abidjan (27.2 per cent and 22.5 per cent, respectively) believed a hardworking person would probably succeed. Of the three samples, more Abidjan respondents believed that such a person would be doomed to failure no matter what action they took. All told, about 32.1 per cent of the Accra employees and 42.2 per cent of the Abidjan employees (compared with 8.8 per cent of the Lagos sample) had little faith in the system. This could be interpreted as an indication that these workers saw their chances of upward mobility as very small, with the predictable consequence of alienation, which many researchers have identified as a key problem in African industry. Alienation does not apply to the worker's relationship with the work environment alone, but also to politics, meaningful social relationships, and so on. It should come as no surprise that many workers reported that they disliked visiting friends.

With regards to the opportunities for advancement available to the ordinary person, again only a small minority in the three samples saw such opportunities as likely to increase to any appreciable extent - the proportion being greater in the Accra sample (18.5 per cent) than in either Lagos (13.4 per cent) or Abidjan (6.9 per cent). Nevertheless, more respondents in Lagos and Abidjan felt that opportunities were improving to some degree, perhaps as a result of recent gains made under the World Bank and IMF-supervised adjustment programmes in both countries. However, more respondents in Abidjan and Accra (45.7 per cent and 46.2 per cent, respectively) did not think that there had been any improvements at all, believing that opportunities had remained the same. A surprisingly large proportion of the Lagos sample, however (24.1 per cent) thought that opportunities were decreasing greatly.

Generally, it would appear that the majority of employees saw opportunities either as static or decreasing, a conclusion that is consistent with the reality of West African countries. More people are being born, more are migrating to urban centres, yet social facilities and employment opportunities are either static or deteriorating. This is hardly a social climate that makes for optimism and hope for the future.

Finally, respondents were asked whether or not they would choose their present occupation if they they had the chance to start all over again. Predictably, most said they would not. Only a tiny minority, less than 8 per cent of the entire sample, reported that they would choose to do what they were doing at the time of the study.

So far in this chapter we have examined several social factors that affect wage employees in the urban environment. We have looked at their salient needs, focusing mainly on housing and modern appliances and consumer items that can be considered essential to urban living. Similarly, we considered their leisure activities and attitudes to life in general. As will be argued later, these social factors have important bearings on the employee's job performance. We turn now to specific job factors.

Job Factors

Specific factors attached to the job and the work environment play an equal part in the determination of the employee's behaviour. One potential shortcoming of the social action perspective is that, in criticizing and moving away from the technological implications approach, it studies work behaviour only in terms of factors *outside* the work environment: the temptation to suspend analysis at the factory entrance poses a real danger. However, it is now commonly accepted that both work and non-work factors are relevant in any analysis. Fox (1971) discussed the experience of work itself, cultural values and ideologies, the values of sub-cultures and certain characteristics of modern industrial consumer-oriented society and determining 'work philosophies', and sees them as transmitted by family, community and work groups. In analysing work behaviour in the West African environment, it is also crucial to integrate work with non-work factors. The aspirations and expectations that are formed by the employee's membership in the larger society are greatly affected by experiences in the work situation. Experiences in the factory system modify or alter the original orientation, and in turn affect life outside work. Thus both spheres are very closely interconnected. The examination of both sets of factors will provide a complete picture of the causes of the pattern of behaviour that the employee displays. Having considered some social factors in the preceding section, we now consider some specific factors in the job environment.

Job Satisfaction

More than most job-related factors, job satisfaction has been a favourite subject of study for industrial sociologists and psychologists alike. A commonly encountered argument in West African industrial circles is that job satisfaction is a luxury that workers in this part of the world can ill-afford. What matters, the argument goes, is that the individual has a job that provides a means of earning a living. Nothing could be further from the truth. It is in the interests of everyone that the work an individual does provides an avenue for happiness as well. Work need not be seen as drudgery, an unpleasant task that is necessary only to ensure the individual's existence and must be avoided in any way possible. This is precisely what Karl Marx meant when he spoke of labour being alienated, a phenomenon that does not stop in the workplace, but spreads to affect other aspects of the worker's life. Job satisfaction is thus the conceptual opposite of alienation. It has been shown repeatedly that workers are satisfied to the degree to which they feel secure in their economic circumstances and to the degree that their efforts are rewarded; to the extent to which they enjoy their relationships with their peers; to the degree to which they feel the risks to their physical safety are both predictable and minimized; to the extent to which they feel their work is challenging and genuinely skilled rather than tedious and simplified; to the degree to which they enjoy some opportunities for personal development, and feel that they have a say in the way things are done.

These are conditions that an enlightened management can fulfil at minimum costs, both in human and material terms. It is evident that job satisfaction is very closely related to the individual's social characteristics, and more significantly to the prevailing working conditions. Research findings from the industrialized countries, especially the United States, show that most industrial workers, contrary to theoretical arguments, report that they are satisfied with their jobs (Blauner, 1960). Results from the developing world have not been so clear cut, although an influential line of thought is Inkeles and Smith's (1960) 'industrial man hypothesis'. This hypothesis states that workers exposed to an industrial environment will adjust to it quickly everywhere. Form (1973) argues that workers, regardless of their skill and job routines or the complexity of plant technology, are generally satisfied with factory employment and their specific jobs, although he concedes that minor variations in satisfaction should occur according to the extent of industrialization in a country. We would therefore expect some measure of satisfaction from the employees presented here. As mentioned previously, job satisfaction for this study was measured by a modified version of the Job Descriptive Index (JDI). The index comprises five dimensions designed to cover as thoroughly as possible the various factors that influence the worker's attitudes and behaviour in the workplace. These dimensions are satisfaction with work, with pay, with opportunities for promotion, with co-workers and supervision.

It has been said that job satisfaction varies with the degree of technological complexity of the operation involved. Workers engaged in large-scale mass production operations, of which vehicle-assembly plant workers are the classic example, are said to suffer low job satisfaction, while independent craftsworkers, who control the pace of their own work and are responsible for the complete production process, are said to enjoy high job satisfaction. Blauner (1960) found that, for modern workers, job satisfaction is roughly proportional to the prestige of one's occupation in the workplace and in the wider society, the control a worker has over the physical and social environment, pace of work, decisions affecting work and the relations with work-mates on and off the job. We will now now focus on the dimensions of work satisfaction, which merit further discussion as they shed much light on the attitudes and opinions of the respondents to several aspects of their job situation.

Work

As stated earlier, all the workers chosen for the sample were involved directly in the production process. The three firms from which these respondents were selected are mono-product organizations making different brands of the same product. About three-quarters of the total sample were machine operatives whose operations kept the flow of work going at a regular pace, while the rest supplied materials or were engaged in packaging operations. In the course of doing these jobs, they have developed opinions and attitudes concerning the physical work they are engaged in. Workers were asked to react to simple statements with 'Yes' if they agreed, 'No' if they disagreed or 'Dont know' if they could not make up their minds. First, the greater majority in Lagos and Accra thought their job was a good one (68.1 and 77.2 per cent, respectively). Even though more than half of the Abidjan respondents (59.5 per cent) considered their jobs good, it is noteworthy that a fairly large proportion (31.8 per cent) could not make up their minds. A possible explanation for this can be found in the fact that in Abidjan the really high prestige jobs are in government ministries and parastatals. These are the places where important decisions are made and these government jobs are far more attractive to native Ivorians than factory or manual jobs. It is not surprising that among this same Abidjan sample, 43 per cent believed their jobs are not respected compared to 41.6 per cent who thought otherwise. Similarly, slightly more than half of the Lagos and Accra samples thought their work respected. This is a crucial factor in worker motivation. We tend to be proud of work that has the respect of other people. In West African countries the doctor, for instance, is a highly respected professional. One would have expected that in a non-technological environment machine operatives would receive adequate respect, yet only a small majority believe their jobs are respected in society. There are psychological consequences for individuals who hold the opinion that their jobs are not respected - they tend to dislike what they are doing and are prepared to leave should another opportunity arise.

A great deal of the literature suggests that machines have robbed workers of the variety and joy of working, thus making most jobs routine and frustrating, a contention that has been substantiated largely by the responses from our three samples of workers. The largest proportion of respondents in the three samples - 44 per cent (Lagos), 46.2 per cent (Accra), and 39.3 per cent (Abidjan) regarded their jobs as routine. That is, they were engaged in the same tasks day and in day out. Even though their jobs were routine, most respondents did not think them frustrating - 47.2 per cent (Lagos), 57.1 per cent (Accra), 43.9 per cent (Abidjan). This is, however, not a unanimous attitude as a sizeable percentage - 30.6 per cent of the Lagos sample, 22.8 per cent of the Accra sample and 22.5 per cent of the Abidjan sample reported that they found their jobs frustrating. Job frustration could prove costly to a company if the proportion of dissatisfied individuals should increase. Nevertheless, despite the relatively large number of employees who thought their jobs routine or frustrating, most respondents thought that their work was useful - 80.6 per cent (Lagos), 68.5 per cent (Accra), 71.7 per cent (Abidjan). In the three samples the proportion of those who had no opinion outweighed the number who thought their jobs were not useful. The fact that most respondents thought that their work was useful implies an acceptance of the basic goals of their establishments. They believed that their work contributed to the total good of the company and that of the society. This is an important source of satisfaction, as studies have shown that workers report high job satisfaction if they perceive the product of their work as serving important functions for consumers. Thus Turner and Miclette (1962) reported that assembly workers attached great importance to their role in producing a needed, high quality product. Similarly Nord (1968) reported that furniture assemblers voiced strong dissatisfaction with management 'cheapening' the product. Along the same lines Terkel (1972) and Heilbroner et al. (1973) reported that many employees are frustrated by the knowledge that their products are trivial in importance and may even be dangerous to the user. Even though many of the respondents, especially those in Abidjan, believed that their work was not given the recognition and respect it deserved, they did believe that they were in some way making a contribution to society. Similarly, most of the employees did not think their repetitive and routine jobs, which require relatively few skills and limited judgement, were in any way simple. Most respondents in the three firms evidently believed that their work was complicated and required some technical expertise. It should not be surprising, therefore, that many of them - 27.7 per cent (Lagos), 22.8 per cent (Accra), 43.4 per cent (Abidjan) - thought that their work was not accorded the respect it deserved.

Pay

Pay is a basic aspect of the work situation. For most employees, and especially those in poor developing economies, pay may be the most important aspect of wage employment and enables the worker to fulfil important obligations outside the work environment. Pay is important to employees in the United States as well. Nord (1977) quotes several researchers who have documented the importance of the economic aspects of work for many contemporary workers. Wool (1973) observed that many individuals (for example, the 20 million workers holding non-farm jobs that pay under $2.50 per hour) do not have their lower needs satisfied. Tansky (1969) observed that 'The economic pay-off from work may frequently be the main focus of concern rather than rewards stemming from prestige or intrinsic content of work' (pp. 54-5). Fein (1976) concluded similarly 'What is really demeaning about low-level skill jobs is that workers in these jobs cannot earn enough to achieve the level of living to which they aspire.' This is particularly true of West Africa where studies have shown that pay is ranked very high in terms of overall satisfaction compared with other factors, and in a situation of widespread poverty and deprivation pay will assume even greater importance. In discussions with respondents, wage levels featured very prominently and responses to questions about satisfaction with pay were revealing. To put it briefly, the responses indicate a marked dissatisfaction with pay among respondents in all three cities: 64.4 per cent in the Lagos sample, 87.5 per cent in Accra, and 70.7 per cent in Abidjan found that their pay did not cover their normal expenses. This is particularly disturbing because salaries and wages in the industrial sector tend to be higher than in other sectors in the region. Many respondents said their salaries were not adequate for their normal expenses: 50.5 per cent (Lagos), 68.5 per cent (Accra), and 41.6 per cent (Abidjan) stated that they could barely live on their income. Some 73.1 per cent, 78.8 per cent and 67.5 per cent in each sample respectively, said that they deserved more pay. These workers considered that they were paid poorly in comparison with managers, who according to one worker, 'sit down in the office all the time doing nothing'. These employees see themselves as the ones who produce the profits, yet they receive the least in terms of benefits. Not surprisingly then, 63.5 per cent of the Lagos respondents, 41.8 per cent of the Accra respondents and 57.2 per cent of the Abidjan respondents thought they were underpaid. This question of dissatisfaction with pay has been a perpetual source of antagonism in West African industry. A great deal of time is lost in disputes over pay, a situation that is bound to continue for as long as workers at the lower skill levels consider themselves worse off in the distribution of organizational benefits.

Promotion

While job satisfaction depends to a large extent on the amount of pay the employee receives and how fair this is considered to be, it also depends on the opportunities available for employee development. When taking up a job, employees expect to move up the occupational ladder, mainly through promotion, which brings with it more money, more responsibility and prestige. However, where individuals perceive that opportunities for such upward movement do not exist or are minimal, dissatisfaction is inevitable. With regards to promotion as a dimension of job satisfaction, the responses among the employees interviewed differed in certain respects. For instance, a very small majority of the Lagos respondents reported that they had good opportunities for promotion (42.1 per cent, compared with 39.8 per cent who thought otherwise). The Accra sample contained more respondents who thought they had the opportunity for promotion - 51.1 per cent, compared witht 15.2 per cent who thought such openings did not exist.

However, it is significant that a large proportion (33.7 per cent) of the sample could not decide whether there were opportunities for promotion or not. If it is assumed that the latter group thought negatively, their combination with those who reported an outright negative response on promotion opportunities will make the total sample virtually divided equally. In the case of the Abidjan firm, most respondents could not decide (37 per cent) while a slightly smaller percentage (34.7 per cent) said they thought that there were opportunities for promotion in their firm. When the opposite statement is examined, we find that the responses discussed above are largely substantiated. A majority of the sample thought that their opportunities for promotion were limited (40.7 per cent for Lagos, 53.8 per cent for Accra and 50.3 per cent for Abidjan). Undoubtedly, most of these workers placed little store on their chances of gaining promotion. This is a realistic appraisal of the situation, as openings above the semi-skilled operative level are relatively few. This means that only a tiny minority will eventually make it to supervisory level. Nevertheless, only a small proportion in the three firms - 29.6 per cent (Lagos), 8.7 per cent (Accra), and 19.7 per cent (Abidjan) believed they had a no-hope job. This implies that, although promotional prospects were limited, people still hoped for promotion, and in fact the majority in the three firms reported that promotions were based on ability, believing that anyone who worked hard enough would be promoted solely on merit. While this may be a comforting thought, promotions are not commonplace, as most of the Lagos and Accra samples suggest. Only 11.1 per cent of the Lagos respondents and 23.4 per cent of the Accra respondents reported regular promotion exercises in their firms. A much larger proportion of the Abidjan respondents (47.4 per cent) reported regular promotions compared with 23.1 per cent who stated that there were no regular promotions and 29.5 per cent who could not decide.

Supervision

Supervision is another aspect of the job situation that is very important to employee satisfaction. It is important to the realization of organizational goals as well. The supervisor or foreman is 'the man in the middle', who stands between the low-level employees and management. He is often in direct personal contact with subordinates, for whom his actions have a distinct significance. The way in which he carries out his functions strongly affects the attitudes and performance of those under him. Supervisory behaviour, according to Bass and Barrett, (1973) can be reduced to two factors - consideration and initiation. According to them, the considerate supervisor tends to emphasize concern for subordinates' opinions on matters of importance. Although he has been given authority over subordinates, he is willing to equalize power to decide upon appropriate courses of action. On the other hand, the highly initiating, directive supervisor insists on maintaining standards, sees that subordinates work to full capacity, offers new approaches to problems, emphasizes the meeting of deadlines, makes his attitude clear and decides in detail what should be done and how. Both types of supervisors, and others in between, have various advantages and disadvantages, a subject to which we shall return in due course. What do the respondents think of their supervisors - and here we must bear in mind that this attitude is an important variable in the determination of performance? The responses indicate that the initiating or directive type of supervisor is the most usual type. For instance, only a small proportion of employees - 38.4 per cent (Lagos), 31.5 per cent (Accra) and 15 per cent (Abidjan) reported that their supervisors asked for their advice. The implication is that for the majority of respondents, especially those in Abidjan, either the supervisors believe the workers to be ignorant and unable to contribute any meaningful advice or that work has already been so organized that it is not necessary to seek anybody's advice. Whatever the reason, the predominance of the directive type of supervisor is again supported by the fact that only a moderate proportion of the total sample believed that their supervisors were not hard to please (44.9 per cent for Lagos, 52.6 per cent for Accra, and 35.8 per cent for Abidjan). Indeed, it is hard to please superiors who believe they already know the answer to every problem. Nevertheless, most respondents believed that their supervisors were prepared to praise good work. Similarly most respondents, the highest proportion being in the Lagos sample (69 per cent), reported that their supervisors knew the job very well. Only 52 per cent of the Abidjan sample and 53.8 per cent of the Accra sample thought that their supervisors knew the work well, while the others were largely undecided. Nevertheless, a significantly smaller segment of the three samples - 31.3 per cent (Lagos), 15.2 per cent (Accra), and 31.2 per cent (Abidjan), thought their supervisors were bad.

Co-workers

The employee who carries out duties in the work situation does not do so as an individual but as a member of a work group. Modern work organization makes it imperative that several individuals combine their efforts before production can take place. The crucial importance of the influence of the work group on individual work behaviour was recognized in the 1930s *human relations approach* led by Elton Mayo. Mayo saw work as being dependent upon a distinct social system that satisfies the basic need 'to belong' and which determines productivity. The work group, apart from carrying out officially assigned duties, also serves the psychological needs of its members in several ways. Blunt (1983) identified five ways in which the group does this. First, groups develop norms or standards of behaviour that members comply with to various degrees. The degree of conformity depends on the extent to which the individual wishes to establish a position in the group and be accepted by group members, the extent to which conformity helps achieve objectives or those of the group, and the pressures brought to bear by other members of the group. Of course there are individuals who are basically 'loners' and who do not subscribe to the various norms that the group may establish regarding how work is done. However, observational data indicates the predominance of conforming individuals because in the long run it is in their interests to do so. Secondly, members may obtain psychological support from their group through the sense of belonging, and the comfort and security it provides through shared interests and views. Thirdly, the group helps to reinforce common values and beliefs. Fourth, work groups help facilitate communication and help to test reality. Thus the group provides an ideal testing ground for its members' ideas and behaviour, as it is psychologically safe. However, Blunt notes further that the ability of the work group to carry out these functions will depend on its cohesiveness. Group cohesiveness, in turn, is determined by the strength of the attraction it has for its members. Members of the same group work in close proximity and develop criss-crossing relationships with each other. In the course of everyday operations they develop subjective evaluations of other members of the group and these subjective evaluations are an important dimension in the employees' general job satisfaction. An employee who has a pleasant relationship with workmates is likely to be a happier worker than one who ignores workmates and in turn is ignored by others. We were interested in the attitude of the sample of employees to their workmates. The largest proportion of the Lagos employees (87 per cent) believed that their co-workers were intelligent people, an evaluation shared to a lesser degree by the Accra and Abidjan respondents (44 per cent and 54.9 per cent, respectively). A sizeable proportion of respondents (36.4 per cent for Accra and 30.1 per cent for Abidjan) thought their co-workers were not intelligent compared with only 7 per cent for Lagos. It could be inferred from these figures that the work groups on the shop floor in these two firms are probably not as cohesive as the Lagos groups. However, with regard to carrying out official duties, the consensus in the three firms was that co-workers were not slow. A slightly larger proportion of the Accra sample (35.9 per cent) believed that their co-workers were indeed slow, a recurring problem on the assembly line where a number of slow workers can cause delays and pile-ups. Again, unlike the other two samples, more of the Accra respondents (38.6 per cent compared with 28.7 per cent of the Lagos sample, and 20.8 per cent of the Abidjan respondents) reported that they thought their co-workers were stupid. Clearly the cohesiveness of the various work groups in the Accra firm was suspect, since most of the respondents had negative attitudes to their workmates. Responses to the other items revealed the same pattern. Most of the Lagos sample (79.2 per cent) reported that they thought their workmates were responsible people. (Responsibility here implies that they can be entrusted with further work obligations and be expected to perform creditably well.) A smaller majority of the Abidjan sample (50.3 per cent) thought along the same lines, with a fairly large proportion of the sample (33.5 per cent) not making up their minds. Of the three samples the Accra sample had the smallest proportion of respondents perceiving their co-workers as responsible - 46.7 per cent as against an almost equally large proportion (31.5 per cent) who thought their workmates were not responsible. Again it can be inferred from this distribution that many of the Accra respondents were of the opinion that their workmates were unable to cope with more work responsibilities, a factor that again points to a lack of solidarity among the work groups in this firm.

In terms of the performance of actual physical work, most respondents in the three firms believed that their co-workers were not lazy. However, this generalization masks significant differences between the firms. By an overwhelming majority (72.7 per cent) the Lagos respondents thought their co-workers were not lazy, compared with only 11.6 per cent who thought otherwise. Presumably, most workers were performing their allotted tasks without holding up the assembly line and causing inconvenience to others. Similarly, a large majority of the Abidjan sample (63.6 per cent) believed their co-workers were not lazy, although a larger proportion (28.9 per cent) than in the Lagos sample thought that they were. This implies that, while most individuals were able to keep up with the pace necessary to maintain the unbroken progress of the assembly line, some found it more difficult to do so. The nature of assembly-line technology is such that if certain individuals cannot maintain the pace there are pile-ups at particular work stations and consequent delays. Where work groups are in solidarity, a great deal of mutual helping occurs. By this we mean that the faster employees either slow down the speed of their own operations or, where this is not possible, they help out the slower ones. The Accra sample had a slightly larger proportion of employees (45.7 per cent) who thought that their co-workers were not lazy, compared with those who thought they were (36.4 per cent). Here, with a weak group performing different functions, the failings of each employee stand out in stark relief. Thus most of these same respondents, in reaction to the statement 'My co-workers are ambitious' could not make up their minds (44 per cent), compared with a slightly lower proportion (40.8 per cent) who believed their mates were ambitious. There is clearly a lack of understanding of each other in this sample and the reason becomes clear after some investigation. Two groups were identified among the workforce on the factory floor: a group who called themselves 'oldies', i.e., workers who were employed before the government nationalized the firm, and the newcomers, who were mostly young and relatively educated workers. Such a conflict can take many forms, including ethnic ones, and does not allow relatively large groups to develop as everybody is suspicious of everbody else, a situation that the supervisors understand and exploit.

On the other hand, work groups were very strong in the Lagos company and many respondents reported that they met outside work for various social activities. Consequently they tended to approve of each other, as demonstrated by their positive attitudes toward workmates. Not surprisingly, 71.8 per cent of the sample believed that their workmates were keen to improve themselves, compared with 22.7 per cent who thought otherwise. The Abidjan sample fell in between these two samples: most people thought their workmates ambitious (59 per cent) yet a sizeable proportion thought they were not (26.6 per cent). It would appear that, with the possible exception of the Accra respondents, the groups had a positive attitude toward workmates. By and large they thought their co-workers to be intelligent, hard-working and responsible. The Accra sample, on the whole, can be said to be fairly positive, but to a much lesser degree.

When all the dimensions of job satisfaction discussed above are amalgamated, a picture emerges in which most employees reported some degree of overall satisfaction with their jobs, although pay caused the most dissatisfaction. This finding of overall satisfaction is consistent with the findings of numerous other studies. For instance, Form (1973), in a study of four countries differentiated on the basis of levels of industrialization, concluded that most workers report satisfaction with their factory jobs although 'Some differences do appear with increasing industrialization but they are relatively small.' It is possible to argue, as some writers have, that in poor developing countries such as those represented in this study, workers are primarily concerned with making a living, and the question of work satisfaction hardly arises. This is misleading, for human beings try as far as possible to derive some joy from whatever they do. Thus black slaves working under very harsh conditions in the South of the United States developed a particular type of music to ease the pain of each day's existence. However, to express some satisfaction with work does not mean one is necessarily happy with that job. In fact it is possible to express satisfaction with a particular job, as it might be the only one available. The worker has no choice but to adapt as well as possible, thereby deriving some semblance of satisfaction from that particular job. In this respect, satisfaction with one's job will then imply how well adapted the worker is to the work environment. Workers who are well adapted and understand the inner workings of the employing organization will tend to express greater satisfaction than workers who are not so well adapted. Since, as Inkeles and Smith (1960) suggested, most people in all countries quickly adapt to the urban and industrial way of life, we would expect that most people will, to varying degrees, express satisfaction with their jobs.

The relative satisfaction expressed by the sample was further substantiated by their responses to a question about whether they were happy with their jobs. More than half of each of the samples reported that they were happy in their present job, although the proportion of the Lagos sample (51.9 per cent) that expressed this opinion was smaller than the other two (65.2 per cent in Accra, 65.3 per cent in Abidjan). It is significant, however, that a sizeable proportion of each sample said they were not happy, a factor that suggests that it is possible to express satisfaction with various aspects of the job, yet be unhappy with its totality. A possible explanation could be the discrepancy between expectations and the concrete rewards provided by the job. When individuals obtain jobs in modern factories, they expect that many benefits, intrinsic and especially extrinsic, will accrue to them. While conditions within the factory might be fine, the job may fall short of fulfilling expectations and thereby lead to dissatisfaction. Respondents were asked further, if they were to start again, whether they would choose their present semi-skilled occupation. Only a minority in the Lagos and Accra samples (40.7 and 24.5 per cent, respectively) felt they would choose to do the same jobs if they had the opportunity to start again. On the other hand, a majority (51.4 per cent) of the Abidjan sample stated that they would choose the same jobs. The presence of numerous migrants from comparatively poor neighbouring countries could be responsible for this distribution of responses. Several studies on Ivorian workers have indicated a liking for white-collar jobs rather than blue-collar manual or semi-skilled jobs. This partly explains why, in a situation of increasing unemployment, foreigners still obtain factory employment. However, 48.6 per cent of the Abidjan respondents said they would choose other types of jobs. The implication is that most of the workers did not particularly like factory jobs, especially in Lagos and Accra. This was confirmed when respondents were asked what type of work they would choose for the same salary or wage. Most workers stated that they would choose office work, which is clean and quiet. This is an indication of the prevalent orientation in the newly developing countries of West Africa where the demand for jobs is skewed in favour of white-collar jobs. One direct consequence of this has been over-sized, over-staffed government ministries and parastatals, which in the three countries studied here are being trimmed down or rationalized as part of the various adjustment programmes adopted recently. The reason for this preference for white-collar office jobs is simple - people tend to accord more respect and prestige to white-collar workers than they do to even skilled blue-collar employees, who in most cases earn *more* than their white-collar counterparts. It is surprising however, that more employees in the Lagos and Accra samples stated that they would prefer jobs in the *agricultural sector* to factory work if the money was the same. If the financial rewards were equal, it is possible that employees would see farming as an occupation in which they could have more autonomy and control over their own labour, a thing not possible in the rigid factory situation. This explanation, however, does not hold for the Abidjan sample, of whom more people said they would rather work in the factory than on a farm, even when the money was the same. Côte d'Ivoire is a largely agricultural country where, to an even greater extent than in

Nigeria and Ghana, land has been privatized and where large agricultural plantations are the rule. A large proportion of the rural population has been transformed into a rural proletariat to work on these plantations, which are run along the same lines as urban organizations. In these jobs, workers still do not have control and autonomy on the job. It would be infinitely better to be an urban proletarian rather than live in a rural area. Respondents were asked to state what factors would influence them most if they had the opportunity to change their present job.

The distribution of responses reveals some interesting differences in the opinions and feelings of workers in the three firms. Based on the discussion so far, one would expect that all respondents would choose 'more pay' as the major factor in any considered change of job. While this is true for Accra and Abidjan respondents, the Lagos employees placed 'working with an understanding boss' ahead of more pay and 'job security'. The logic of this preference would seem to be that with an understanding boss, the employee has leeway to handle the job the way he or she wants. One respondent commented that 'If the Ogre (the boss) is a good man, then you will enjoy your job and whatever small money you are paid, you will be happy, but a bad Ogre will make life miserable for workers and no amount of money you are paid, whenever you remember you have to face the man, you are worried.' On further probing, it was found that the production engineer was a very difficult individual to get along with, and many junior employees were afraid of him. His favourite trick was to prowl round the factory during the night shift looking for workers who were asleep. Once he found anyone in this situation, the highest punishment meted out was a warning, followed by dismissal if the employee repeated the offence. The majority of low-level workers would want a more understanding superior. Among the Lagos sample, job security was placed second ahead of increased pay. In most poor countries, job security is a major concern of the vast majority of employees. Increased pay was placed third among the sample, while working with friendly co-workers was placed last, with only 2.4 per cent of the sample saying it would be the most important factor influencing their possible choice of job. In this respect the Lagos sample was similar to the Accra sample, and placed working with friendly co-workers last as well. This should come as no surprise in view of the Accra respondents' showing in the preceding section. Nevertheless, the Accra sample had the largest majority (40.2 per cent) choosing more pay as the decisive factor. In this respect they were similar to the Abidjan sample, of whom 34.7 per cent chose increased pay also. This largely instrumental orientation is not peculiar, as evidence from other societies also suggests that most workers will place more pay ahead of other factors when choosing a job. For instance, Goldthorpe *et al.* (1968), in their 'Affluent Workers' study, showed that the skilled workers at the Luton assembly plant chose their jobs, which were dirty, noisy and routine, because of the high pay attached to them. Of course higher pay facilitates the pursuit of other more interesting activities outside work.

'Opportunity for more promotion' was placed second on the list of decisive factors when choosing a job by the Accra respondents. As shown earlier, promotion is an avenue for achieving higher wages and increased social status. Job security and working with an understanding boss were chosen by an equal number of employees. The Abidjan respondents placed work that they really liked second on the list. As noted above, native Ivorians prefer to work in white-collar, preferably government jobs, and could be expected to ascribe a high priority to work of their own choice. Job security came third, while opportunities for promotion was placed last. The major difference between the samples is that the Accra respondents emphasized *extrinsic* rewards as the most important variables to consider in any proposed change of job. The Abidjan sample emphasized money as well, but this was followed by a liking for the job. Finally, the Lagos sample differed from the other two by putting an understanding boss first, a factor that the Accra sample placed fourth and the Abidjan sample placed fifth. These differences could be traced back to existing circumstances, both in the work environment and in society at large. In Ghana, as a consequence of a long period of economic decline, the need for money is overwhelming. In Côte d'Ivoire, the literature suggests that the indigenous population would rather have white-collar, preferably Civil Service jobs, although the need for money still ranked highest. In Nigeria, the massive retrenchments of recent years have left their mark. Workers were concerned with working for a boss or superior who would not constitute a threat to their jobs, while the issue of job security was also crucial and thus ranked second.

Autonomy

Autonomy in the sense in which it is used here refers to the degree of control that the employee exercises over immediate work procedures. The literature usually refers to individuals who have little or no control over the work process as being alienated from that work. According to Blauner (1964), alienation 'is a general syndrome made up of a number of different objective conditions and subjective feelings'. Seeman (1959) identified five dimensions of alienation: feelings of powerlessness, meaninglessness, isolation, normlessness and self-estrangement. It is the dimension of powerlessness that concerns us here. It is defined as 'the expectancy or probability held by the individual that his own behaviour cannot determine the occurrence of the outcome or the reinforcement he seeks'. As Seeman noted, for the alienated person, control seems vested in external forces, powerful others, luck or fate. To determine the degree of powerlessness, we have to examine how far workers can control their conditions of employment, or regulate the work process itself, their pace of work or their working methods. The consensus seems to be that individuals who achieve some measure of control over the job are usually more satisfied and thus less alienated, whereas those manual and semi-skilled workers who have little control over their work procedure are the most susceptible to alienation. This appears to constitute a major problem in West Africa where the majority of industrial employees are in the unskilled, manual and semi-skilled categories. For instance, Ogionwo's (1971) study of Nigerian workers in Port Harcourt found that alienation was 'higher among manuals than non-manuals'. Given this background, the respondents were asked to react to several statements designed to determine the level of control they had over their work.

The distribution of responses showed immediately that lower-level production employees in all three firms perceived that they had very little control over the work process. Every segment of the work process had been so rationalized and routinized that it did not require much mental activity to keep pace with it. For instance, only a very small minority of respondents (a total of 15.4 per cent for the Lagos sample, 13.6 per cent for Accra and 13.8 per cent for Abidjan) reported that they had the freedom to decide what they did on the job. These were individuals not directly involved in the assembly line - individuals who supplied materials or performed a number of other support jobs that could not be further rationalized. Similarly, only a negligible proportion of respondents reported that they had the responsibility to decide how their jobs were done. A striking proportion of individuals were ambivalent, and could not make up their minds, especially in the Lagos and Accra samples (22.7 per cent and 20.7 per cent, respectively). This pattern was also repeated in response to a question about the amount of input the individual had about what happens on the job. This statement is similar to the former one and the pattern of responses is fairly consistent. For the majority of the Abidjan sample, though, there was no such ambivalence: 30.1 per cent clearly perceived their powerlessness in the job situation. However, the large number of employees who expressed no opinion in the Lagos and Accra samples (44.9 per cent and 37 per cent, respectively) could be interpreted in either of two ways. Perhaps these workers were indifferent to the work process, in which case they might have recognized their inability to control the situation and learned to live with it, exhibiting a sort of apathy. Perhaps they had genuinely not thought about the situation. This is a more plausible explanation. Perhaps these young semi-skilled operatives expected to be told what to do and simply act on it without actually thinking that they could achieve more control. When confronted with a statement about amounts of responsibility on the job, they are baffled by it and find that the easiest way out is not to express an opinion.

In some organizations, especially in the developed world, workers are allowed to choose their workmates, especially in dangerous occupations such as coal mining, for example. The underlying objective of this choice is that workers feel more comfortable with people they know than with complete strangers whose capabilities they know nothing about. The assumption, of course, is that such work groups will perform very efficiently. However, for the three firms here, the great majority of respondents reported having a choice as to who their workmates were. Altogether, less than one-fifth of the total sample reported having any hand in the decision as to who would work with them. Related to the choice of workmates is the speed of the work process itself. Assembly-line technology allows little room for individuals to determine the pace at which they work, as the speed of the belt is already predetermined by engineers on the basis of calculations of speeds sufficient to produce the required number of goods in a given time. The distribution of responses support this explanation, as most workers disagreed or strongly disagreed with the statement that they determined the speed with which they work - 47.7 per cent (Lagos), 67.9 per cent (Accra), 68.2 per cent (Abidjan) - with a sizeable number remaining undecided (again in the Lagos and Accra firms, which recorded 34.7 per cent and 24.5 per cent in this category, respectively). Finally, in response to the statement that they were given a lot of freedom to decide how they did their work, a total of 12.5 per cent of the Lagos sample agreed, while 24.4 per cent and 21.3 per cent of the Accra and Abidjan samples also agreed. The majority either disagreed or expressed no opinion. From the discussion so far, it is evident that this category of employees in the three firms had relatively little control over their immediate work processes. Again, this is a major characteristic of assembly-line technology and has led theorists to conclude that alienation is highest under such conditions. Seeman (1972), for instance, has argued that control in the workplace is a major factor in shaping the individual's self-image and feelings of effectiveness. Work over which the employee has no control tends to disrupt the individual's psychological development, since self-image will suffer in the process. A way out of this problem is to involve *all* employees, especially those at the lower levels, in decision-making, and especially in those decisions that concern them directly. This method of decision-making has generated a great deal of interest and is usually referred to as *participative management*. It is to this that we now turn.

Participation

Employee participation refers to a situation in which employees at every level may have a real share in the decisions within a company and therefore share in the responsibility of making it a success. Put in another way, employee participation implies a situation in which some power to influence important decisions in the organization is extended to the general workforce. This is in contrast to the commonly observed situation in which the power to make all decisions rests with management. Where participation exists, several levels can be identified. Wall and Lischeron (1977) identified three levels - local, medium and distant. Local participation involves a situation where workers have the power to influence decisions that affect their immediate jobs. Such decisions, being confined to the shop floor, have little effect on the organization as a whole. Medium participation takes this one step further and involves a broad range of decisions that are normally made by middle management. 'These decisions affect more people in the organization, say a whole department or division, and include such matters as personnel selection and placement, performance appraisal, training and the purchase of equipment and material.' Distant participation, on the other hand, involves participation in decisions that affect everybody in the organization and usually takes place at the highest levels in the firm.

Participation has taken different forms in different countries and a great deal of the literature indicates the relative success accomplished by greater democracy at work. Several specific benefits have been identified as deriving from involving lower-level employees in decision-making. They include improved performance, increased labour efficiency, decreased resistance to technical change and decreased labour turnover.

In the three firms, no type or level of participation was observed. The closest employees came to supplying any input into the decision-making process was through the trade unions. However, the absence of concrete participatory mechanisms notwithstanding, we were determined to seek employees' opinions on participation. They were asked how much say they thought workers should have in respect of five factors: how the work was done; wages and salaries; recruitment and dismissal; days and hours of work; safety equipment and practices. Respondents had a choice of four categories: no say at all; some say; a lot of say; and complete say.

Predictably, the majority of respondents in all three firms wanted employees to have a hand in the making of important decisions in the workplace. However, this needs some qualification. The pattern of responses shows that the respondents thought that some aspects of the work procedure required more employee input than others. Secondly, it would appear that the respondents did not think that employees should have complete say in the running of things. With regards to how the actual work is done, most respondents agreed that employees should have a say. Only a very negligible proportion - 7.4 per cent (Lagos), 9.8 per cent (Accra), and 9.7 per cent (Abidjan) - would *not* want employees to have a say at all. However, subtle differences appear in the degree of influence the respondents thought that workers should have. More of the Lagos and Abidjan respondents (38.4 and 35.8 per cent, respectively) wanted workers to have some say in how their work was done. The implication here is that the final decision should still rest with those who, at present, wield authority. More of the Accra respondents preferred workers to have more input into the decisions governing work procedure. The pattern of responses was similar with regard to wages and salaries. Only a very small minority (13 per cent on average) did not want workers to participate in the making of decisions concerning pay. Again there were differences about the degree of participation. More of the Lagos respondents wanted workers to have complete say (32.9 per cent), most of the Accra respondents wanted them to have a lot of say (59.8 per cent), while most of the Abidjan respondents wanted workers to have just some say (52.6 per cent). Surprisingly, the largest single category among the Lagos respondents (38.9 per cent) wanted employees to have no say at all concerning matters of recruitment and dismissal. Again, this can be attributed to the legacy of recent retrenchments when supervisors had to draw up lists of names from their various sections for sacking. These workers believed that a number of people were sacked unfairly, as other workers who were on good terms with the supervisors had complained about them. To a lesser degree, more of the Abidjan respondents wanted workers to have no say (21.4 per cent) in recruitment and dismissals than those who wanted workers to have complete say (11 per cent).

The most interesting responses concerned safety equipment and practices. Evidently employees would want to leave such important decisions to the experts. In all the firms, a large proportion (32.4 per cent for Lagos, 27.2 per cent for Accra and 28.9 per cent for Abidjan) would want workers to have no say at all. Even among those who wanted workers to participate in safety matters, relatively few (an average of 20 per cent) wanted them to have complete say.

Thus, we have seen that this category of employees reflects the majority of industrial employees in West Africa who lack any measure of autonomy on the job and have very little say in the way things are run in their workplaces. This is an unfortunate situation, for existing evidence suggests that a great deal is gained when some measure of control and participation is granted to employees. Numerous surveys have linked enhanced productivity with the practice of participative management. As we shall show, participative management is not an entirely new concept or practice in Africa. It is consistent with traditional work ethics and would result in the release of suppressed talent and energy.

Having discussed the various elements that impinge on the individual's attitude to work, attention will now be focused on individual performance, followed by an examination of hypotheses raised earlier in view of the findings presented so far.

Work Performance

Work performance has been the subject of intensive study by industrial sociologists and psychologists for many decades. This interest is, of course, in consonance with the primary objective of all industrial organizations - the overriding need for profit. It is perhaps stating the obvious that improved worker performance on the job is one of the surest ways for industrial organizations to make a profit. Probably the first systematic approach to the enhancement of worker productivity is the *scientific management* approach spearheaded by Frederick Taylor. Scientific management as a management philosophy brought considerable precision of measurement into the organization of the individual employee's production activities. As Taylor stated, 'Scientific Management involves a complete mental revolution, both on the part of the management and of men. It is a complete change in the mental attitude of both sides towards their respective duties and towards their opponents.' With his 'time and motion' techniques, Taylor and his associates were able to increase productivity significantly and, at the same time, pay productive workers higher wages. Again, according to him, 'When we went to the Bethlehem Steel Company, we found 400-600 men at work in the yard and when we got through (three and a half years later) 140 men were doing the work of 400-600 and these men handled several millions of material a year.' Although Taylor's ideas and practices were successful in raising productivity, they were largely unacceptable during his time and he spent a great deal of time defending them. The Machinists Union, which at that time was in the forefront of the battle against Taylorism, opposed the philosophy on several grounds. According to them, scientific management:

1 tends to deprive the worker of thought, initiative, achievement and joy in. . .work;
2 tends to eliminate skilled crafts;
3 is destructive of mechanical education and skill;
4 tends to deprive the worker of the possibility of learning a trade;
5 condemns the worker to a monotonous routine;
6 dwarfs and represses the worker intellectually;
7 tends to destroy the individuality and inventive genius of the worker;
8 stimulates and drives the workers to the limits of nervous and physical exhaustion and overstrains them;

9 tends to reduce the worker to complete dependence on the employer - to the condition of an industrial serf.

Although scientific management was roundly condemned and has been overtaken by other more 'humane' management philosophies, it still retains some relevance for developing economies - a point to which we shall return.

Job performance here is conceptualized as how effectively a worker performs tasks when judged against existing standards in the work environment. This implies not only how much effort is put in at work but also how effectively duties and responsibilities are discharged. Furthermore, it concerns adjustment to the work situation and relations with supervisors and co-workers. A worker who is high on all these counts will, no doubt, be a good producer. The performance ratings of the workers in the sample were obtained from company annual reappraisal exercises in which each individual employee is rated on a list of items and which we standardized for the three firms in Lagos, Accra and Abidjan. Although the evaluations were quantified, the items on which they were appraised - the amount of knowledge required by the job; the quality and quantity of work; adaptability; initiative; punctuality; supervision; co-operation - require examination before we examine the pattern of distribution.

Although the appraisal system is subjective, it can be considered acceptable for this study because it was used officially in the firms concerned for promotion and other related company exercises. According to interviews with several employees in each firm, it would appear that workers had confidence in these exercises, but for different reasons. In Abidjan, where employee confidence was strongest, the workers all agreed that their evaluation system was fair. The major reason they gave was that the predominance of expatriate managers minimized problems of ethnicity and favouritism. This proved a difficult issue to verify, however. As far as these employees were concerned, they believed that they were rated fairly, that they received the ratings they deserved. Employees in Lagos and to a lesser extent Accra thought similarly that the appraisal exercises were fairly accurate. In the Lagos firm the procedure was fairly straightforward and involved the employee. The evaluation was done by the employee's immediate supervisor, after which the form was passed to the departmental manager's office where the employee was invited to read the appraisal and to sign it, if satisfied. Disagreements occurred frequently, in which case a more senior staff member, who was familiar with the employee, was invited to conduct a re-appraisal. Charges of favouritism are fairly common, although everybody in the end accepts the outcome of the exercise. The procedure was similar in Accra, although the general attitude to performance evaluation here was one of indifference. A few employees suggested that the system was adequate, but could be improved. Very few people, however, had any concrete suggestions for improvement. On the other hand, management in the three firms believed that the various appraisal exercises were fair, accurate and impartial. The consensus was that hard-working employees are usually accurately identified and evaluated, and that it was usually the less hard-working individuals who complained the most.

The pattern of distribution of employees in the various evaluation categories listed above was revealing. Most categories had a preponderance of workers evaluated as 'average'. In contrast, comparatively few employees were rated either 'below average' or 'outstanding'. With regards to the level of knowledge essential to work, the Accra sample had more respondents (58.2 per cent) who were rated above average than respondents who were rated average (37.5 per cent). The reason for this is simple enough. The Accra sample contained more educated people carrying out tasks that require minimal expertise. However, more respondents in Lagos (68 per cent) were rated average than in either of the other two samples (37.5 per cent in Accra, 48.2 per cent in Abidjan), while more Abidjan employees (5.8 per cent) were rated outstanding (in Lagos the figure was 1 per cent, in Accra 4.3 per cent). Since limited technical expertise is required for this type of job, experience and interest assume prime importance. The experience of performing the same task every day makes the worker quite adept at it and interest levels tend to rise, dispelling boredom and indifference. Another reason why the Accra sample contained more people in the above-average category is the fact that the Accra firm had a higher proportion of long-serving employees who had mastered the techniques required by the job. The firm has been able to retain this group of employees primarily because alternative employment opportunities are rare in Accra, whereas in Lagos and Abidjan some measure of occupational mobility is still possible. In these circumstances, although workers in the Accra sample had become very experienced at their jobs, the question of whether they were interested in the job is another matter, and one that will be explored in due course.

The quality and quantity of work are essential elements in assessing a worker's productivity and are areas to which managers pay special attention. These elements, more than any other, determine a company's profitability. Usually standards are laid down toward which every employee must strive. Those who are unable to comply with them are dismissed. Workers attain the stated standards quite easily and the difference between a committed and hard-working employee and a 'mediocre' one is that the former keeps working *beyond* the quota. The 'mediocre' employee stops once the quota is reached and idles away the time. However, the usual practice is to allow the job to fill the amount of time available. Thus if workers are to produce 20 units in six hours, the production of the 20 units will be staggered so it occupies the full six hours. This was observed in all three firms and represents a conscious restriction of output. That fact notwithstanding, more workers in the Lagos and Accra firms were rated average in terms of quality of work (71.3

and 70.7 per cent, respectively). The Abidjan sample was more evenly distributed with 38.7 per cent rated above average compared with 29.3 and 26.9 per cent for Accra and Lagos. Similarly, the Abidjan sample had more people rated outstanding (2.3 per cent). The picture is similar for quantity of work, except that a small but significant number of employees in the three firms were evaluated as outstanding - 1.4 per cent (Lagos), 1.6 per cent (Accra), 2.3 per cent (Abidjan).

Initiative is another important element in the worker's performance. No matter how strong and diligent, a worker who lacks initiative cannot be an efficient and effective producer. The common argument is that modern industrial work deprives the worker of the opportunity to use initiative since the work has been so rationalized that there is virtually no room for its application. This might be true to some extent, but in the day-to-day operations in the factories in this study, ample opportunities arose for employees to display initiative. Workers who were interested in and committed to their jobs would not find it difficult to apply initiative whenever the need arose, whereas uninterested and uncommitted employees would be indifferent and 'go by the book', a very common phenomenon in government-owned establishments in West Africa. The ratings for initiative in the three firms are depressingly similar. Most people were rated as average - 94.4 per cent in Lagos, 83.2 per cent in Accra, 85.5 per cent in Abidjan - with more people rated below average than outstanding in the three samples. The Lagos firm even had more people rated below average than above average, (2.8 as against 1.4 per cent). The Accra sample had no outstanding employees but 2.7 per cent rated below average. The Abidjan firm had more workers rated below average (3.5 per cent) than the other two firms, while having more rated above average (10.4 per cent). While the sample could not be said to be entirely lacking individuals with initiative, it cannot be said to have had them in abundance. Most employees just managed to get by.

Supervision is related to the issue of initiative. It is only logical to assume that employees who do not hesitate to apply initiative as soon as the need arises require less supervision than those who lack or refuse to use initiative. Employees react to supervision in many ways, depending on their experiences. In Africa cultural values can and do affect workers' reaction to supervision as the quotation from Gutkind (1968) illustrates:

> I did not like the Foreman because he did not treat me well. All the time I was working there he was always looking at me and trying to find fault with me. He was telling me how I should do the work but he did not speak to me well and he told me that unless I improved my work he would fire me. I told him that I was trying to do my work well and that I wanted to learn and that it was his duty to teach me. Then one day he was very rude to me and told me that people of my tribe should go back to the country and grow food because that is all we are good for. He was always comparing me to other people in the factory who were better workers. He said that it was due to the fact that they were of a different tribe. I spoke to the Manager about my complaint and he told me that I was a good worker and not to pay any attention to those comments. Then one day the Foreman complained that I had not washed my hands properly and I became angry with him. We had a quarrel and he told me that he despised people of my tribe so I left.

Conflicts such as the one described above are bound to occur in all work situations where some people have authority over others. Nevertheless, if handled poorly, such conflicts can be time-wasting and costly to the employing organization. Properly motivated employees would need less supervision and thus save the firm money. The respondents in the sample were evaluated with regard to their relationship to their supervisors. It is remarkable that in both the Abidjan and Accra samples, 6 per cent and 6.4 per cent, respectively, were rated below average compared with 0.9 per cent for

Lagos. This is an indication that a sizeable number of employees in both Accra and Abidjan had problems with their foremen and supervisors, a situation that could be costly. It could lead to increased turnover of experienced employees as Gutkind's example shows, or it could lead to costly delays or even widespread disaffection between employees, supervisors and foremen, a situation that would clearly result in poor productivity. Nevertheless, it is gratifying to note that most employees in the three firms were evaluated as average (91.7 per cent for Lagos, 87 per cent for Accra and 75.7 per cent for Abidjan). The Abidjan firm, however, had more workers assessed as being above average (17.9 per cent, compared with 7.1 per cent for Accra and 6 per cent for Lagos). The Abidjan and Accra samples contained no employees who were rated outstanding with regards to supervision, compared with 1.4 per cent of the Lagos sample.

The other elements - adaptability, co-operation and punctuality - are also important to the employee's overall performance. Adaptability and co-operation are crucial if team-work and team spirit are to be built up and maintained. The majority of the sample in the three firms were rated average on their adaptability and co-operation. Similarly, with regards to punctuality, most employees were rated average. When all the elements are taken into consideration the picture that emerges shows the majority of employees in all three firms as being rated average on most of the dimensions of job performance. When the ratings were converted into scores and computed, remarkably similar mean scores were recorded for the three samples. The Lagos sample recorded a mean of 17.35 (standard deviation of 4.4), the Accra sample had a mean of 17.5 (standard deviation of 1.7) and for the Abidjan sample the mean score was 18 (standard deviation of 2). It can be imputed from these figures (based on company appraisal records), that the typical semi-skilled employee in the three firms in Lagos, Accra and Abidjan involved in making consumer items, is an average producer. That is, the employee puts in just enough effort to satisfy company requirements. Beyond meeting this official requirement, the employee exhibits no additional interest. This finding calls into question the commitment of this category of employees, a subject to which we shall return shortly. We are, however, not implying that *all* employees in this category are mediocre producers, because no doubt some individuals are highly efficient and hard-working. The data above confirms this. What is disturbing is that the data also suggests that such hard-working individuals are in a minority. For company prosperity and larger societal development, the majority of workers must be above-average producers. Thus the problem that confronts us here is how to explain the prevailing levels of performance. As we suggested earlier, of the two factors that determine employee productivity - ability and motivation - the latter seems to be most problematic. So the question is, how can industrial workers be motivated toward higher productivity? We examined two sets of factors that have significant implications for employee behaviour at work. These are the social factors that operate outside the work environment and influence the employee both inside and outside the work situation. The second set of factors is concerned with the immediate work environment itself. Both sets of factors interact and, to a very large extent, determine the employee's behaviour at work - the employee's performance. We now turn our attention to exactly how these factors relate to performance.

Job Satisfaction and Employee Performance

The main hypothesis has been that employee performance is dependent on job satisfaction. Satisfaction was very broadly defined to include pay, promotion prospects, the task itself, relationship with co-workers and supervisors. It was hypothesized that the higher the degree of satisfaction the worker derives from the job, the better the performance. When the scores for both variables were correlated, the relationship was found to be .0149 for Lagos, .1237 for Accra and .2807 for Abidjan. Thus a positive relationship can be seen to exist between job satisfaction and work performance, although the data presented in Pearson correlation co-efficients showing the relationship between variables suggests that it is a very weak one. Although the hypothesis cannot be rejected, we must nevertheless admit that the statistical support is fragile, especially in the Lagos sample. We can take consolation in the fact that this finding is neither strange nor new. Since 1932, when Kornhauser and his associates first examined the relationship between job satisfaction and performance, numerous studies have shown that it is an extremely complex relationship. However, Bass and Barrett (1973) suggest that, after more than 40 years of study, scholars at least agree that there seems to exist a consistent low positive relationship between job satisfaction and performance. They gave the example of Vroom, who after reviewing 20 studies relating satisfaction to performance, found a median correlation of +.14. What is not under contention is the fact that job *dissatisfaction* has been found to result in cost-increasing employee behaviour, especially low productivity and a propensity to strike. For our purposes here, therefore, we want to accept that employees who feel some satisfaction with their jobs will tend to perform better at work than those who do not derive much satisfaction from their employment. Since the relationship between satisfaction and performance is a complex one, other independent variables - age, educational levels, place of birth, duration of current employment, control at work, participation, leisure - were computed against job satisfaction, which we regard as an intervening variable between these other variables and job performance.

Age and Job Satisfaction

A low positive relationship is recorded for the Lagos (.2076) and Accra (.2137) samples with regards to age and satisfaction. That is, the older the employee the more satisfaction felt in the job. The same is not true for the Abidjan sample, where a very low inverse relationship (-.0501) was recorded. The implication here is that the older the worker, the less the satisfaction with the job, and conversely, the younger the worker the more job satisfaction reported. The situation in the Lagos and Accra firms could either be attributed to older workers having adapted better to the situation or having resigned themselves to fate, whereas in Abidjan older workers with more responsibilities and obligations found little cause for satisfaction in their semi-skilled jobs. Here also, younger workers, mostly migrants who considered themselves fortunate to have a job, reported higher job satisfaction.

Education and Job Satisfaction

In the Abidjan sample a low positive relationship (.2845) was computed between the educational level attained by each worker before employment, and job satisfaction. In this case, the higher the education of the employee, the greater the job satisfaction reported. This finding corroborates the earlier one in which younger workers in the Abidjan firm reported higher job satisfaction. The point here is that young, fairly well-educated employees felt a greater degree of satisfaction with their semi-skilled factory jobs than the older, less well-educated individuals. This finding was again substantiated by the earlier response of the Abidjan respondents to the question 'If you were to start again, would you choose your present occupation?' More than half of the sample (51.4 per cent) said yes, compared with 40.7 and 24.5 per cent of the Lagos and Accra samples, respectively. Thus if a slight majority of the Abidjan employees were to choose these jobs again, there is no reason to suppose that they did not derive a measure of satisfaction from their jobs at the time of the study. For the Lagos and Accra samples, very low inverse relationships were recorded, (just -.0165 and -.0459 for Lagos and Accra respectively). Unlike the situation in Abidjan, the better-educated persons in Lagos and Accra felt *less* job satisfaction. That is, educated employees performing semi-skilled, repetitive operations tended to report less job satisfaction. Evidently, such employees felt they were over-educated for their current occupational levels, and this affected their attitude to the job. However, the absence of viable alternatives made it impossible for them to move to other employment. This is apparently not a new phenomenon in a number of West African countries, where there is a discrepancy between labour supply and demand. The tremendous growth in general education has not been matched by concomitant increases in job creation, and as more educated individuals are thrown onto a labour market where there are too few jobs, they will have to lower their sights and consider less desirable jobs. It is unlikely, however, that these over-educated individuals would feel very satisfied with the types of jobs that are available to them in the current employment situation, as the data demonstrate.

Place of Birth and Job Satisfaction

Earlier we had hypothesized that rural-born employees who had migrated to the city in search of work would, when they succeeded in finding jobs, be more satisfied with them than urban-born employees. Data from the three samples confirm this hypothesis, although to various degrees. Low positive relationships (.1459 and .1498) were recorded for the Lagos and Accra samples with regards to rural birth and job satisfaction. A much stronger relationship (.4416) was computed for the Abidjan sample. This is not surprising, since most of the employees in Abidjan were migrants from the Côte d'Ivoire hinterland or from neighbouring countries. Generally, it would appear that the aspirations and expectations of rural migrants are likely to be lower than those of urban-socialized individuals. Urban life inculcates the desire for many consumer goods that a semi-skilled worker's wages simply cannot fulfil. Migrants on the other hand, at least initially, have comparatively more limited wants - for a job, food and shelter, and so on. When they obtain jobs, these initial wants are fulfilled, and they believe they are getting a good deal and report higher job satisfaction. Another factor that must be considered here is the gap between rural and urban incomes. Evidence suggests that rural incomes are lower than urban incomes in most African countries, and a migrant who obtains urban employment experiences a significant increase in earnings, and this is as much a source of satisfaction as any other.

Basic Needs and Job Satisfaction

Housing was taken as a typical basic need of employees in urban employment. When correlated with job satisfaction, a strong positive relationship (.7279) was recorded for the Abidjan sample. That is, the better the housing arrangement the employee enjoys, the greater the job satisfaction. When compared with Lagos and Accra, housing is much better in Abidjan and the strong relationship computed is not surprising. Better-housed employees feel happier at work. A fairly strong relationship (.4022) was also recorded for the Lagos sample, while a relatively low, but positive relationship, was computed for the Accra sample (.2415). The data presented above confirms the hypothesis that the more basic needs a job fulfils, the greater the job satisfaction for the employee. Conversely, when an employee thinks that needs and wants are not being met by the rewards of the job, dissatisfaction is likely to occur. Housing is, however, a major problem in most West African countries. The implication is that many workers throughout the region are poorly housed and the loss in productivity can only be imagined.

Duration of Current Job and Satisfaction

The greater the number of years the individual spends doing the same job, the greater his/her experience and skill. We expected the more experienced and skilled workers to feel more satisfied with their jobs. This hypothesis was verified by data from Abidjan where a fairly strong relationship (.5983) was found between length of employment and job satisfaction. A very low positive relationship (.0878) was also found for the Accra sample. However, an inverse relationship existed for the Lagos sample. That is, the more the years on the job, the less satisfaction reported. Again, it is a very weak negative relationship. Experienced workers want to move up the employment ladder and earn more money and prestige, which the bureaucratic authority system makes very difficult. This gives rise to feelings of immobilization, a belief that experience and skills are not appreciated or rewarded, and job *dissatisfaction*.

Control at Work and Satisfaction

Very close supervision has been found to be correlated with low productivity and absenteeism at work. As Katz and Kahn (1953) noted, studies reveal that frequent and detailed instruction and close checking of the subordinate's work is not the best method of supervision: on the contrary, such close supervision actually reduces productivity. We hypothesized that workers who had some control over their work tasks would tend to report higher job satisfaction than those who had to obey instructions all the time. Statistical evidence supports this hypothesis. By far the strongest relationship was recorded for the Lagos sample (.7712). Employees who are periodically called upon to use their initiative tend to report higher job satisfaction. Relatively low positive relationships were also found for the Abidjan (.3012) and Accra (.2581) samples. That is, individuals whose jobs gave them some freedom to determine the flow of work felt a higher degree of job satisfaction; conversely those individuals whose jobs did not allow any display of personal qualities tended to feel more dissatisfied. This, of course, depends on the extent to which the task has been rationalized. The greater the division of the work process into smaller segments, the less the amount of control the worker will be called upon to exercise. This is the reality of most assembly-line type jobs.

Participation and Satisfaction

Participation is closely related to the type of control in the workplace. Participation, as noted earlier, concerns the amount of influence employees have on decision-making at work. There is a fair amount of evidence that the exercise of discretion and responsibility increases satisfaction at work. Coch and French (1948) found that factory workers who participated in decisions about a change in production, accepted change more readily than those without a voice in the making of such decisions. We then hypothesized that employees who had a say in decision-making in the workplace would report higher job satisfaction. Correlating both variables, fairly strong positive relationships were found for the three samples. The relationship was strongest in the Lagos sample (.5646) and weakest in Accra (.3226). This finding is an indication that the increased democratization of the workplace could lead to a happier and more satisfied workforce who have influence in making decisions, at least those decisions that influence their immediate work tasks.

Leisure and Satisfaction

Leisure is a variable that operates outside the work environment and which has a great influence on work behaviour. It refers to the unobligated activities of the employee during free time away from work. We expected that employees who pursue interesting and satisfying leisure would be positively oriented in their attitude to work. Correlating leisure with satisfaction produced a very strong positive relationship with regards to the Abidjan sample (.8207). Here evidently, leisure was taken seriously and it influenced job satisfaction positively. A fairly strong relationship was also computed for the Lagos sample (.4840), while a low positive relationship was found for the Accra sample (.2466). The implication here is that individuals whose leisure activities offered them rest and relaxation after work tended to express higher satisfaction at work. Individuals who, for one reason or another, were unable to enjoy their leisure-time activities tended to report low job satisfaction or outright dissatisfaction.

Conclusion

> It is not the absence of economic man that has put tropical Africa so far behind the great societies of Europe, Asia and America. He lives in Africa today, as he has for millenia, and will eagerly serve African society as he has other societies when his presence is recognized and his tremendous energies freed to work for the common good.
>
> William O. Jones

The underlying assumption here has been that in West African industry there is a significant discrepancy between possible and actual levels of worker performance. Although this gap exists worldwide, it is so large in Africa as to affect productivity significantly - hence the frequent complaints about the low performance of African industrial workers. One way of closing that gap is by introducing more sophisticated production technology, an option that is severely circumscribed by a chronic shortage of investment capital. This shortage of capital in turn drastically limits any programmes of industrial modernization and expansion, and the remaining option is therefore to make more efficient use of the existing stock of human resources. Perhaps the only way of doing this is to focus attention on those factors that influence the worker's behaviour at work, especially the subjective factors that exercise a great influence on performance.

These factors include:

1 the skill or qualifications of the worker;
2 the intensity of effort in the labour process, or the intensity of work;
3 the innate abilities of the worker, i.e., physical and mental energy.

With regard to worker skills or qualifications, we can conclude, on the basis of the three samples surveyed, that these West African workers were not in any way deficient. As was shown, the samples were made up of young, reasonably well-educated individuals. Their jobs - what Bhagavan (1979) called 'repetitive partwork', require little technical skill or knowledge and are thus easily grasped. Bhagavan characterized these jobs thus:

> All these forms of partwork characterize a pre-automatic stage of manufacture. These operations are, for technological or economic reasons, not mechanized. The operations which the worker performs are completely determined by the design and layout of the process of the conveyor belt or the machine. The worker is an element in the assembly line - he has to repeat operations according to the pace set by the plant - the workplace is fixed and he cannot leave his position without interrupting the whole process. He is a left-over of automation, which makes him even more an integral part of the plant.

Two considerations arise from this characterization. First, as the work is largely repetitive, little skill or knowledge is required for its execution, and it can be argued that most of these workers, with their present levels of education, had the requisite intellectual capacity to cope quite comfortably with these tasks. Neverthess, the employment of over-educated individuals for such semi-skilled jobs is likely to become an increasing trend. It is also to be expected that as economies stagnate further in the face of unabated urban population growth, and as the educational system produces more and more graduates, more people will have to lower their sights with regards to employment. This is very likely to lead to increasing alienation at work, which is the second consideration to be borne in mind.

With regards to the physical and mental energies of workers, there is no evidence of any inherent incapabilities in the three samples studied here - these West African workers are as capable as any other group of workers anywhere in the world of carrying out the tasks required of them by their factory employment. Yet as the data have shown, productivity remains fairly low (a confirmation of past complaints). This is where the third subjective factor becomes relevant. The problem thus lies with the amount of effort that the worker invests in the job. It is also in this area that the differences exist between Japanese, North American or Swedish workers and African workers. Workers in these other countries or regions are highly motivated to invest a great deal of effort in their work - hence the higher output per head. What is wrong with African workers?

Job Expectations and Aspirations

Two major issues must be addressed here, both of which are linked directly with the worker's quality of working life and hence with job satisfaction. These issues are first, the worker's expectations and aspirations and the possibility of them being fulfilled by the job, and secondly, the type of managerial strategies currently operating in West African industry. Before we address these issues some comment is necessary about the whole concept of the worker's quality of working life and its relevance or irrelevance to the West African context.

It is not uncommon in African industry, even among government officials, to encounter the view that it is a waste of time and scarce resources to deal with the quality of working life, as most workers can be considered extremely fortunate to be employed at all. The consensus is that attention should be focused on other more urgent problems, notably employment creation. This is an unfortunate state of affairs and, according to Cherns and Davis (1975), is the result of a misreading based on false historicism:

> Because industrialization was accompanied in the past by a widespread decline in the quality of working life, it has become accepted that the price of industrialization is alienation as well as dense urbanization. Yet neither of these consequences is an inevitable concomitant of industrialization. Furthermore, the currently present symptoms of dissatisfaction in advanced countries appear to be largely associated with and more than partially the outcome of, steps taken to advance the efficiency of work organizations. Again the ills are seen as part of the cost of efficient operation. Costs they are, but paradoxically uncosted: necessary costs they are not. Newly industrializing countries need no more follow the road of 'scientific management' than they need begin their industrialization with James Watt's steam engine.

The concept of the quality of working life does not refer to any undue state of luxury for workers but is essentially a new term for a number of old issues that have long been of interest to philosophers, theologians, social scientists, workers and employers.

> It is a broad term that can embrace every conceivable aspect of work ethics and work conditions. . .objective measure of working conditions, workers expressions of satisfaction and dissatisfactions, managerial concerns about efficiency of output and broader considerations of social cohesion and stability. (Merton, 1977)

The concept thus implies that the needs, concerns and interests of all participants in the work organization are taken into consideration in work design and redesign. Frequently, however, the needs and interests of workers become more or less submerged under the organization's over-riding goal of higher productivity. The 'quality of working life' perspective therefore serves mainly to highlight those needs and interests of the worker. According to Walker (1975):

> The elements of relevance to the worker's quality of working life involve the task, the physical work environment and the social environment within the plant - the administrative system of the enterprise and the relationship between life on and off the job. The factors bearing upon the relative importance attached to these elements include demographic considerations, socio-economic status, culture and personality, politics and ideology and the 'situation' which is concerned with technology and size of the plant. . . .An effective approach to the enhancement of the quality of working life must explore the weight of these factors on the worker's attitudes towards all the elements that make up his working attitude.

In return for an enhanced quality of life that derives directly from an enhanced quality of *working* life, the employer can expect employees to react positively to exhortations for increased productivity. Thus under certain circumstances we can expect enhanced quality of working life to lead to higher worker productivity.

Based on the data presented in this study, from observations and discussions with numerous workers, it can be concluded that the quality of working life among West African semi-skilled factory workers is very low. On balance, it is evident that they do not benefit to any significant degree from their industrial jobs in terms of the fulfilment of their aspirations and expectations. Unfortunately, management in the region makes little effort to determine how workers' satisfaction could be brought about. The reason for this is not far-fetched. In West Africa, as in most of Africa, unemployment is a serious problem, and employers can afford to get rid of any worker who is not able to maintain the required pace. Of course, most employees can put in enough energy to fulfil the quotas required by the company, but a great deal is lost because most employees are not committed to their employment. It must be noted here that there is no doubt that most workers in West Africa are committed to industrial work and the way of life it engenders. In this sense, one cannot but agree with Moore (1963) that 'Commitment involves both performance of appropriate actions and the acceptance of the normative system that provides their rule and rationale.' As noted earlier, a manifestation of this commitment to industrialism is the acceptance by an increasing proportion of West Africans of permanent urban residence, employment in the formal sector of the economy where possible, and a reluctance to return to the rural areas and the old ways. It was observed, however, that there was a relatively widespread disenchantment with specific jobs. Workers complained, not about wage employment *per se* but about the particular jobs they had. The general atmosphere in all the factories visited was of a feeling of exploitation on the part of the workers. There was a feeling of not having an equitable share in the profits generated by their labour. This is the fundamental reason for low productivity in West Africa. Workers do not see any reason why they should work beyond the bare minimum required to retain their jobs. They do not, in any way, share the management goal of enhanced productivity being beneficial for the organization and for society at large. Work is done mechanically with the sole objective of earning money and nothing more. This situation was summarized by Cervinka (1964):

> As long as the means of production are produced, distributed, exchanged and consumed with the interest of a certain class in mind, and as long as the finished product again becomes the property of only one part of society, increased labour productivity will concern only the owners of the

> means of production, while the producers will only be indirectly interested because of their need for subsistence. This indirect interest is not sufficient incentive for increases in labour productivity.

Thus, unless the prevailing situation is changed, low productivity will continue to be a major problem. Initially, the search for a solution to the problem lies in considering the orientation that these workers have to their jobs and the influence of organizational factors, notably the style of management.

On the basis of the data presented, we want to suggest that the predominant orientation among these workers is instrumental. Given the widespread background of poverty throughout much of West Africa, this type of orientation is inevitable. People tend to regard their jobs, not as an end in themselves or as a 'central life interest', but as a means to other ends. In the present circumstances, the end toward which most workers labour is money that will enable them to fulfil responsibilities. In this regard, job satisfaction becomes an expression of a complex balance between what the worker gives to and receives from the job. If the worker believes that what is given is more than what is received, the consequence is dissatisfaction, and restriction of output. Unfortunately, this is a fairly common belief amongst workers. For industrial workers in West Africa there is a palpable disparity between the expectations they bring to the job and the reality they encounter there.

Another factor that further compounds this feeling of exploitation is the influence of reference groups. In all working-class areas throughout West Africa there is a conglomeration of different groups. One of the most eminent is that comprising local self-employed individuals, who could be referred to in Marxist terms as the 'petty bourgeoisie'. More often than not these are individuals who were previously in formal employment, but who have set up businesses of their own. In spite of their relative 'success', however, they usually continue to live in the poor areas. These are the individuals who serve as reference groups to most industrial workers. To a large extent, these workers' aspirations are influenced by these reference groups, against whom these workers evaluate themselves. As Chapman and Volkman (1952) argued, one way in which the social environment might determine the level of aspiration of a given individual would be through the knowledge of the achievement of groups whose status or ability the worker could assess. This implies that the worker's perception of the relative achievement of reference group members will constitute the point of comparison conditioning the level of satisfaction. This factor helps account for the frequently expressed preference of workers in West Africa for self-employment. With reference to the worker in Lagos, Peace (1974) argued that:

> A combination of his experience in the established Yoruba township and the new environment of the Lagos suburb, Ikeja or Agege townships, points to the open mobility of the entrepreneur, the independent man. . . .It is the successful independent man, not the industrial manager or Civil Servant, alongside whom the wage earner lives and establishes interpersonal relationships, who is the key reference point in the cognitive map of the industrial employee and is the one with whom he can most clearly identify.

This characterization, with slight modifications, could be extended to other West African cities. Another factor that adds to the unappealing situation of the worker is the lack of job security and the very minimal possibility of promotion. Job security is a very important consideration for industrial workers worldwide. However, it assumes critical dimensions in the developing areas where unemployment means a grave crisis for the worker. This is particularly so because of the absence of social security arrangements in most of West Africa. The motivation to hang on to any job in spite of very unpleasant working conditions is very powerful. Programmes that tend to increase the job security of these workers would be welcomed enthusiastically. Related to this is the problem of promotional prospects. Promotion is a means through which the employee's share of profits are enhanced and is thus very desirable for most workers. Its desirability notwithstanding, the fact is that only a very limited number of semi-skilled and even skilled workers are likely to be promoted, as there are always fewer opportunities for promotion than there are potential candidates. This is a factor many workers recognize. As Chinoy (1952) aptly noted, two continuous ladders of promotion seem to have emerged in modern industry. One ladder is open to workers and is short, with few rungs, usually ending - at best and for only a handful of men - with foremanship. The other, which is open to those who start as technicians or white-collar employees in the office, is longer and may eventually lead to top levels of industry. It is not surprising that most workers, realizing the impracticability of their jobs leading anywhere, talk about leaving to set up 'something of their own'. Unfortunately, a great many of them never manage to save enough capital to do this. The culmination of all these factors - lack of job security, poor chances of promotion to a higher-paid job and a generally poor quality of working life for the majority of workers - is a feeling of alienation. This is quite pervasive and arises from a feeling of powerlessness to exercise any control over the forces that guide daily life at work. Unfortunately, since work is seen largely in instrumental terms, this alienation is carried over into social life after work. In fact a great deal of frustration is carried from work to the home. As we saw, leisure, which could otherwise have served as a safety valve, cannot perform this critical function for the simple reason that leisure facilities do not exist in most lower-class areas. Furthermore, workers cannot afford to pursue any leisure activity that involves a financial outlay. The end result is a very tenuous attachment to work, a relationship Beynon (1973) described as a 'brittle bond'. It is a bond based on the need for cash from which all moral commitment is totally absent and can easily be broken.

Management Style

The second major issue involves the style of management in West African industry. The industrial organization is a system of interrelated activities of people who are performing a task that has been differentiated into several distinct subsystems. By performing a portion of the task they are integrated into the effective performance of the system. In this system, management stands as the pivotal group. Its functions are: maintenance of organizational communications, which include charting the organization, specifying the work to be done and the personnel required; secondly, securing the essential services of individuals, which includes bringing people into co-operative relationships with the organization and eliciting services from them; finally, the formulation and definition of the purposes and objectives of the organization. In performing these vital functions, different forms or styles of management have developed, corresponding to the level of industrial development of the society. In West Africa, the management styles in the three factories visited were basically similar. Within these organizations, maximum authority is exercised by top managers with very limited delegation of authority at the lower levels: among shop-floor workers, the power to exercise control over even the most routine of day-to-day matters is very limited. Thus, management control is usually very strong, a factor that also conditions the type of supervision exercised by the foremen. It is a very close system of supervision based, as we discovered, on the outmoded assumption that the workers need close supervision if anything is to be achieved. Most of the procedures involved in a task are spelled out by the foreman, who constantly checks up to see how things are being done. Even though workers have developed various means of adapting to the system of supervision, it is still a feature that many of them find irritating. Day and Hamlin (1964), hypothesized that close supervision could result in increased aggression on the part of the worker. One would expect that such a system of supervision results in:

1 an increase in the amount of verbal aggression towards the supervisor;
2 a decrease in productivity;
3 an increase in verbal aggression towards co-workers;
4 an increase in dissatisfaction with the work situation.

In the final analysis, the combination of unfulfilled aspirations and expectations with an alienating management control system, does not in any way make for a committed discharge of duties and helps explain the problem of low performance in West African industry.

How then can this situation be reversed? A very simple solution would be to recommend wage increases for industrial employees. The belief in management circles is that there is a positive relationship between high monetary reward and productivity. However, for very many economic reasons, the wages of workers have to be kept as low as possible. Nevertheless, the issue must be addressed of whether more money can serve as a sufficient incentive to motivate workers to higher productivity. To some extent the answer is affirmative. Many workers in the three cities said that more money on the job would improve their quality of life significantly. Increased earnings would enable them to meet their various obligations and then pursue other more interesting activities outside work. The underlying assumption here is that people do not work for the sake of work itself but for the money it brings. The long-term effects of higher wages would be positive for the workers and society as a whole. As W. E. Moore (1961) stated:

> Where labour is in excessive supply, low wages make eminently good economic sense for the individual employer, eminently bad sense for the economy as a whole if an expanding internal market is desired. Moreover, there is a kind of vicious circle that links low wages and low productivity. Given any kind of market orientation on the part of workers, uneconomically high wages may be the correct transitional strategy. Thus, minimum wage laws, with governmental subsidy if necessary, may not be as silly as conservative economic doctrine would indicate.

Whatever wage increases are instituted, however, they must be linked with the result of the employee's work. What is called for here is the introduction of a payment method that will act as a gearing device for effort and enable workers to earn extra money for extra effort. This linkage of payment with effort is generally absent in West African industry where workers are paid flat rates for working a certain number of hours per day (what industrial analysts call 'time rate'). We advocate a modified version of the traditional 'piece rate' system. Under this system workers are guaranteed a certain minimum income, with the opportunity to earn extra money by putting in extra effort. Workers who feel they require more money would have the incentive to work harder and longer than those who think otherwise, and would still be able to maintain their jobs without problems.

It must be said that higher wages alone might not be enough to evoke the desired behaviour from workers. Workers must not be in constant fear of losing their jobs. Where a constant burden of fear exists, as in West Africa, workers cannot develop their skills and ideas sufficiently. It is difficult to be innovative in a situation of job insecurity. Perhaps West African industry can learn from the Japanese experience, in which security of tenure is rigidly upheld and compensated for by fierce worker loyalty to the company. Declining industries transfer workers to other divisions or companies where labour is needed. Even companies that are not large or particularly diversified sometimes subcontract labour to firms that need it. With the employee's future more or less secure, it is not surprising that Japanese workers have among the highest productivity per head in the world, and would rather work than take vacations.

Job security is linked with the type of management control system that is employed. As noted earlier, in much of West African industry, all power to influence decisions rests with management, while at the lower levels close supervision is the norm. The worker is made more or less into a passive object, a part of the machine. However, it is a fundamental fact that no one is happy in a situation where there is no opportunity to exercise even the smallest amount of control. The existing management control system, although apparently successful (the companies make profits) is not very compatible with the sociocultural environment of West Africa. It is an alien, imported management system that generally distances the workforce, deprives it of the essential meaning and satisfaction that daily tasks should provide, and thus results in indifferent performance. The threat of unemployment often functions to maintain a more or less stable labour force and adequate productivity, although exhortations by management and government for increased productivity are not likely to have much effect. What is required is a management system that allows the participation of the entire workforce. According to Heron (1948), if decisions are to be carried out effectively, the decisions themselves must be made on the basis of all available thinking that is pertinent. He argued further that we cannot hope to have an effective industrial organism comprised of distinctively separate units distinguished as the 'workers' and the 'thinkers'. Nor can we 'expect teamwork from 90 per cent of the team members if we insist on telling them that their function is to work, ours to think'. What West African industry needs is the institution, if possible by legislation, of employee participation in decision-making. This is a system that falls short of total workers' control but which involves employees at all levels in the making of important decisions. This type of management system is particularly relevant to West Africa for several reasons. First, employee participation is not in conflict with private or social ownership of capital. Rather it postulates that, in a productive activity where a group of workers co-operate in a joint effort, the right to control and manage that effort rests with all members of the group. That is, capital assets can be owned by individuals or anyone else outside the enterprise, but the owners cannot decide on the complex human activities that constitute production. Rather, they can only expect adequate compensation for the use of these assets. Added to the basic compatibility between private property and employee participation is the fact that participative management, as it is sometimes called, is also very compatible with the traditional work ethic of West African people. The following list includes some of its more relevant aspects:

1. the employer-employee relationship was non-existent in the traditional work situation;
2. all adult males were eligible to participate in decisions with regard to community work;
3. in joint working parties, despite the fact that certain individuals were known to be stronger and to contribute more towards the achievement of group goals, they received no extra material reward from the group beyond the recognition of their contribution through praise;
4. in family and community work there was no division of the group into those who gave and those who carried out orders. The decision about how any particular work should be carried out was entirely that of the group.

These features are still very prevalent in the traditional sector, which continue to exert a strong influence on West African urban-based industrial workers. Finally, a great deal of the existing literature on the subject indicates the success of employee involvement in managing enterprises. Among the advantages to be derived from this system are increased performance, increased labour efficiency, decreased resistance to technical change, and decreased labour turnover. A great deal of creativity and innovativeness stands to be uncovered by this involvement as well. A practical example of this is the statement made by a Chinese worker who suggested that:

> The goals of this technical revolution are proposed by the different workshops, with a view to improving quality, raising labour productivity, guaranteeing safety and reducing working tension. It is generally in these areas that technical innovations are made. In this way we are able to discover new raw materials, new techniques, new technologies, new equipment and new methods. We are always looking for the techniques that offer the most advantages and cause the least waste. Technical innovations are a very important means of developing industry.

There is no doubt that the interaction of higher wages and the involvement of all levels of employees in making important decisions will contribute immensely towards overcoming the persistent problems of low productivity in West African industry.

Bibliography

Africa Confidential (1987), 28, 15, July.

Africa Confidential (1987), 28, 18, September.

Ake, C. (1981), *The Political Economy of Africa* (London, Longman).

Arrighi, G. (1968), 'Labour Supplies in Historical Perspective', in G. Arrighi and J. Saul, *Essays*.

Arrighi, G. and Saul, J. (1973), *Essays on the Political Economy of Africa* (London, Monthly Review Press).

Barnard C. (1947), *The Functions of the Executive* (Harvard University Press).

Bass, B. and Barrett, G. V. (1973), *Man, Work and Organisations* (New York, Allyn and Bacon).

Bennett, R. (1974), 'Orientation to Work and some Implications for Management', *The Journal of Management Studies*, 11, pp. 149-62.

Bennett, R. (1978), 'Orientation to Work and Organizational Analysis: A Conceptual Analysis, Integration and Suggested Application', *The Journal of Management Studies*, 15, 2.

Berg, E. J. (1965), 'The Development of a Labour Force in Sub-Saharan Africa', *Economic Development and Cultural Change*, XIII, 4, July, pp. 394-412.

Berger, P. (1964), *The Human Shape of Work* (New York, MacMillan).

Beynon H. and Blackburn, R. M. G. (1972), *Perceptions of Work* (Cambridge University Press).

Beynon, H. (1973), *Working for Ford* (Harmondsworth, Penguin).

Bilton, T. *et al.* (1981), *Introductory Sociology* (London, MacMillan Press).

Bhagavan, M. (1979), *Interrelations between Technological Choices and Industrial Strategies in 3rd World Countries* (Uppsala, Scandinavian Inst. of African Studies), no. 49.

Blauner, R. (1960), 'Work Satisfaction and Industrial Trends Society', in W. Galenson and S. Lipset (eds) *Labour and Trade Unions* (New York, Wiley).

Blauner, R. (1964), *Alienation and Freedom* (Chicago, University of Chicago Press).

Blunt, P. (1983), *Organizational Theory and Behaviour* (London, Longman).

Brayfield, A. and Crochett, W. (1955), 'Employee Attitudes and Employee Performance', *Psychological Bulletin*, 52, 5.

Brown, J. A. C. (1958), *The Social Psychology of Industry* (Harmondsworth, Pelican).

Brown, R. (1973), 'Sources of Objectives in Work and Employment', in J. Child *Man and Organization* (London, Allen and Unwin).

Capelle (1950), in UNESCO *Social Implication of Industrialization and Urbanization in Africa South of the Sahara*, 1956.

Carlson, J. (ed.) (1983), *Recession in Africa* (Uppsala, Scandinavian Inst. of African Studies).

Cervinka, A. (1964), 'Wages and Labour Productivity in the System of Planned Direction of Czechoslovak Economy', in T. Dunlop and J. Diatchenko (eds) *Labour Productivity* (New York, McGraw Hill).

Chapman, D. and Volkman, J. (1952), 'A Social Determinant of the Level of Aspiration', in Swanson *et al. Readings in Social Psychology* (New York, Holt and Co.).

Cherns, A. B. and Davis, L. E. (1975), 'Assessment of the State of the Art' in L. E. Davis and A. B. Cherns (eds) *The Quality of Working Life*, vol. 1 (New York, MacMillan).

Chinoy, E. (1952), 'Tradition of Opportunity and the Aspirations of Automobile Workers', *American Journal of Sociology*, 57.

Chirsman F. P. (1976), *Attitude Psychology and the Study of Public Opinion* (Pennsylvania State University Press).

Chrisnall P. M. (1975), *Marketing, a Behavioural Analysis* (London, McGraw Hill).

Cohen, P. C. (1966), 'Social Attitudes and Sociological Inquiry', *British Journal of Sociology*, 17, p. 341.

Cohen, R. (1976), 'From Peasants to Workers in Africa', in P. C. W. Gutkind and I. Wallerstein (eds) *The Political Economy of Contemporary Africa* (London, Sage).

Dawson, J. L. (1963), 'Traditional Values and Work Efficiency in a West African Mine Labour Force', *Occupational Psychology*, 37, pp. 209-18.

Day, R. C. and Hamlin (1964), 'Some Effects of Close and Punitive Styles of Supervision', *American Journal of Sociology*, March, pp. 499-510.

De Briey, (1955), 'The Productivity of African Labour', *International Labour Review*, August/September, pp. 119-37.

Drucker, P. (1950), *The New Society* (New York, Harper Bros.).

Dumazedier, J. (1960), 'Current Problems of the Sociology of Leisure', *International Social Science Journal*, 4.

Durkheim, E., *The Rules of Sociological Method*, ed. G. Catlin, trans S. Solovary and J. H. Millet (New York, Free Press).

Economist Intelligence Unit (1987-8), *Country Profile, Nigeria.*

Ejionye, U. A. (1984), 'Industrial Relations of the 1980s', in P. Ejiofo and V. Aniagoh (eds) *Managing the Nigerian Worker* (Lagos, Longman), p. 195.

Elkan (1956), *An African Labour Force*, vol. 7 (Kampala, East African Inst. of Social Research), p. 8.

Elkan (1960), *Migrants and Proletarians* (London, Oxford University Press).

Erikson, K. (1986), 'On Work and Alienation', *American Sociological Review*, 51.

Ford, H. (1922), *My Life and Work* (New York, Doubleday, Page and Co.).

Form, W. H. (1973), 'Auto Workers and their Machines: A Study of Work, Factory and Job Satisfaction in Four Countries', *Social Forces*, 52, pp. 1-15.

Fox, A. (1971), *A Sociology of Work in Industry* (London, Collier MacMillan).

Frank, A. G. (1967), *Capitalism and Underdevelopment in Latin America* (New York).

Friedman, G. (1961), *Industrial Society* (Glencoe, Ill., Free Press).

Glass, Y. (1961), *Industrial Man in Southern Africa* (Johannesburg, National Institute for Personnel Research).

Gluckman, M. (1961), 'Anthropological Problems Arising from the African Industrial Revolution', in A. W. Southall (ed.) *Social Change in Modern Africa* (London, Oxford University Press), pp. 67-82.

Goldthorpe, J. H. (1966), 'Attitudes and Behaviours of Car Assembly Workers', *British Journal of Sociology*, 17, pp. 227-44.

Goldthorpe, J. H. *et al.* (1968), *The Affluent Worker* (London, Cambridge University Press).

Gouldner, A. W. (1959), 'Organizational Analysis', in R. K. Merton *et al.* (eds) *Sociology Today: Problems and Prospects*, vol. II (Harper and Row).

Gussman, B. (1953), 'Industrial Efficiency and the Urban African', *Africa*, XXIII, 2, April.

Gutkind, P. C. W. (1968), 'African Responses to Urban Wage Employment', *International Labour Review*, 97, pp. 135-66.

Gutkind, P., Cohen, R. and Copans, J. (eds) (1978), *African Labour History* (London, Sage Publications).

Harbison, F. (1964), 'High Level Manpower, Productivity and Economic Development', in Dunlop and Diatchenko (eds) *Labour Productivity*.

Harbison, F. and Myers C. (1959), *Management in the Industrial World* (New York, McGraw Hill).

Heron, A. (1948), *Why Men Work* (Stanford University Press).

Horton, S. and King, T. (1981), 'Labour Productivity: Un Tour d'Horizon', World Bank Staff Working Paper, no. 497.

ILO (1958), *African Labour Survey* (Geneva, 1958), p. 169.

ILO (1981), *First Things First: Meeting the Basic Needs of the People of Nigeria* (Addis Ababa, JASPA), pp. 7-9.

ILO (1982), *Rural-Urban Gap and Income Distribution: A Comparative Sub-Regional Study - The Case of Nigeria* (Addis Ababa, JASPA).

Ingham, G. K. (1967), 'Organizational Size, Orientation to Work and Industrial Behaviour', *Sociology*, 1, 3.

Ingham, G. K. (1970), *Size of Industrial Organization and Worker Behaviour* (Cambridge, Cambridge University Press).

Inkeles, A. and Smith, D. (1974), *Becoming Modern* (London, Heinemann).

Inkeles A. (1960), 'Industrial Man', *American Journal of Sociology*, LXVI.

Katz, D. and Kahn, R.L. (1966), *The Social Psychology of Organizations* (London, John Wiley and Sons).

Kayode, M. O. (1970), 'A Re-Examination of the Concept and Factors Influencing Productivity with Particular Emphasis on Motivation', *Nigerian Journal of Economic and Social Studies*, 12, 1, March.

Kilby, P. (1961), 'African Labour Productivity Reconsidered', *The Economic Journal*, LXXI.

Lewis, W. (1954), *Economic Development with the Unlimited Supplies of Labour* (Manchester School).

Lloyds, P. C. (1967), *Africa in Social Change* (Harmondsworth, Penguin).

Lord Harley (1957), *An African Survey* (London, Oxford University Press).

Mabogunje, A. L. (1980), *The Development Process* (London, Hutchinson Library).

Mannel, S. (1974), *Sociological Theory* (London, Thomas Nelson and Sons), p. 27.

Marx, K. (1906), *Capital* (Chicago, Charles Kerr and Co.).

Maslow, A. H. (1954), *Motivation and Personality* (New York, Harper and Row).

Merton H. (1977), 'A Look at Factors Affecting the Quality of Working Life', *Monthly Labour Review*, 100, 10.

Miller, D. C. and Form, W. H. (1964), *Industrial Sociology* (New York, Harper).

Miracle, M, and Fetter, B. 'Backward Sloping Labour Supply Function and African Economic Behaviour', *Economic Development and Cultural Change*, 18.

Miracle, M. and Fetter, B. (1956), *The Impact of Industry* (Englewood Cliffs, NJ, Prentice Hall).

Moore, W. E. (1963), *Social Change* (Englewood Cliffs, NJ, Prentice Hall).

Nord, W. (1977), 'Job Satisfaction Reconsidered', *American Psychologist*, 32, pp. 1026-35.

Northcott C. H. (1947), *African Labour Efficiency Survey* (London).

Ocho, L. O. (1984), 'Cultural and Environmental Influences on Work Attitudes', in P. Ejcofor and V. Anogon (eds), op. cit.

Ogionwo, W. (1971), 'The Alienated Nigerian Worker: A Test of the Generalization Thesis', *Nigerian Journal of Economic and Social Studies*, 13, 3, pp. 267-84.

Oloko, O. (1983), 'Factors in Labour Productivity', in A. M. Osoba (ed.) *Productivity in Nigeria*, pp. 7-46.

Onitiri, H. M. (1983), 'Productivity and Economic Development', in Osoba (ed.) *Productivity*, pp. 1-6.

Onyemelukewe, C. O. (1966) *Problems of Industrial Planning and Management in Nigeria* (London, Longman).

Onyemelukwe, J. O. C. and Filani, M. I. (1983), *Economic Geography of West Africa* (London, Longman).

Orde-Brown, J. (1933), *The African Labourers* (London).

Osoba, A. M. (ed.) (1983), *Productivity in Nigeria* (NISER).

Parker, S. (1983), *Leisure and Work* (London, George Allen and Unwin).

Parsons, T. (1951), *The Social System* (Glencoe, Ill., Free Press).

Parsons, T. and Shils, L. (eds), *Towards a General Theory of Action* (New York, Harper and Son).

Peace, A. (1974), 'Industrial Protest in Nigeria', in E. de Kadt and G. Williams (eds) *Sociology and Development* (London, Tavistock).

Peil, M. (1972), *The Ghanaian Factory Worker: Industrial Man in Africa* (Cambridge, Cambridge Univ. Press).

Pfefferman, G. (1968), *Industrial Labour in Senegal* (New York, Praeger).

Rao, D. C. (1974), 'Urban Target Groups', in H. Chenery *et al.*, *Redistribution with Growth* (Oxford University Press), p. 138.

Rose, M. (1975), *Industrial Behaviour* (Harmondsworth, Penguin).

Sandbrook, R. (1977), 'The Political Potential of African Urban Workers', *Canadian Journal of African Studies*, XI, 3, pp. 411-33.

Sandbrook, R. (1982), *The Politics of Basic Needs* (Toronto, University of Toronto Press).

Seeman, M. (1959), 'On the Meaning of Alienation', *American Sociological Review*, 24, pp. 783-91.

Seeman, M. (1972), 'The Signals of 68: Alienation in Pre-Crisis France', *American Sociological Review*, 37, pp. 385-402.

Seidman, A. (1986), 'The Need for an Appropriate Industrial Strategy to Suport Peasant Agriculture', *Journal of Modern Africa Studies*, 24, 4, pp. 547-8.

Sellassie, S. O. (1980), 'The Social Implications of the Lagos Plan of Action for the Economic Development of Africa', paper written for the Third Conference of African Ministers of Social Affairs, Addis Ababa.

Shaw, T. M. (ed.) (1982), *Alternative Future for Africa* (Boulder, Colorado).

Sik, E. (1974), *The History of Black Africa*, vol. III (Budapest, Akademiai Kiado), pp. 33-4.

Silverman, D. (1970), *The Theory of Organizations* (London, Heinemann).

Soper, T. (1958), 'Labour Migration and Labour Productivity: Some Aspects of Experiences in East, Central and Southern Africa', *Race Relations Journal*, XXV.

Spengler, J. (1961), 'Theory, Ideology, Non-Economic Values and Politico-Economic Development', in R. Braibanti and J. Spengler (eds) *Tradition, Values and Socio-Economic Development* (London, Cambridge University Press).

Streeten, P. (1984), 'Self-Reliant Industrialization', in C. K. Wilber (ed.) *The Political Economy of Development and Underdevelopment* (New York, Random House).

Sutermeister, R. A. (1976), *People and Productivity* (New York, McGraw Hill).

Taylor, F. W. (1949), *The Principles of Scientific Management* (New York, Harper and Row).

Terkel, S. (1972), *Working* (New York).

Timberlake, L. (1985), *Africa in Crisis: The Causes, the Cure of Environmental Bankruptcy*, ed. J. Tinker (Earthscan).

Todaro, M. P. (1973), 'Income Expectation, Rural, Urban Migration and Unemployment in Africa', in ILO *Employment in Africa - Some Critical Issues* (Geneva), p. 49.

Tovoedjere, A. (n.d.), *Poverty: Wealth of Mankind* (International Institute for Labour Studies).

Vanek, J. (1970), *The General Theory of Labour Managed Market Economies*, pp. 4-5.

Vroom, V. H. (1964), *Work and Motivation* (New York, John Wiley and Sons).

Walker, K. F. (1974), 'Workers' Participation in Management Problems, Practice and Prospects', *Bulletin of the International Institute for Labour Studies*, 12, pp. 3-35.

Wall, T. D. and Lischeron, J. A. (1977), *Worker Participation* (London, McGraw Hill).

Weber, M. (1947), *The Theory of Social and Economic Organization* (Oxford University Press).

Woodward, J. (1958), *Management and Technology* (London, HMSO).

Woodward, J. (1965), *Industrial Organization: Theory and Practice* (London, Oxford University Press).

Wool, H. (1973), 'What's Wrong with Work in America? A Review Essay', *Monthly Labour Review*, March, pp. 38-44.

World Bank (1981), *Accelerated Development in Sub-Saharan Africa, an Agenda for Action* (Washington, DC).

World Bank (1977), *Prospects for Developing Countries* (Devt. Policy Staff, Washington DC).

Yesufu, I. M. (1982), *The Dynamics of Industrial Relations: The Nigerian Experience* (Ibadan, Ibadan University Press).

About the Author

Dr Austin N. Isamah was educated at his home university of Ibadan, Nigeria, from where he obtained a Ph.D. in Sociology in 1984. Formerly lecturer in the Department of Sociology at Ibadan, Dr Isamah is currently ACARTSOD Senior Research Fellow. He has published a number of articles on wage employment, employee participation and the Nigerian Labour Movement, as well as on trade unionism in Cameroon.